Oedipus at Colonus

The Focus Classical Library
Series Editors • James J. Clauss and Michael Halleran

Hesiod's Theogony • Richard Caldwell • 1987
The Heracles of Euripides • Michael Halleran • 1988
Aristophanes' Lysistrata • Jeffrey Henderson • 1988
Sophocles' Oedipus at Colonus • Mary Whitlock Blundell • 1990

Forthcoming
Euripides' Medea • Anthony Podlecki • 1991
Lucretius' On The Nature of Things • Walter Englert • 1991
Apollonius' The Argonautica • James J. Clauss • 1991
Sophocles' The Women of Trakhis • Richard Martin • 1991
The Homeric Hymns • Susan Shelmerdine • 1992
Vergil's The Aeneid • Patricia Johnston • 1993

The Focus Library of Medieval Women
Series Editor • Jane Chance

Christine de Pizan's Letter of Othea to Hector • Jane Chance • 1990
Margaret of Oingt • Renate Blumenfeld-Kosinski • 1990

Forthcoming
St. Bridget of Sweden Writings • Julia Bolton Holloway • 1990
14th Century German Convent Literature • Rosemary Hale • 1991
Hrotsvit of Gandersheim Legends • Katharina Wilson • 1992
Hildegard of Bingen: On Natural Philosophy and Medicine • Margaret
Jackson • 1992
Magdelana of Freiburg: Selections • Kate Greenspan • 1992.

Sophocles' *Oedipus at Colonus*
Translated with Introduction, Notes
and Interpretive Essay

Mary Whitlock Blundell
University of Washington

Focus Classical Library
Focus Information Group, Inc.
PO Box 369
Newburyport MA 01950

Cover: Calyx-krater depicting Oedipus at Colonus, reproduced courtesy of Graham Geddes.

This book is published by Focus Information Group, Inc., PO Box 369, Newburyport, MA
01950. All rights reserved. No part of this publication may be reproduced, stored in a re-
trieval system, or transmitted in any form or by any means, electronic, mechanical, by photo-
copying, recording, or by any other means, without the written permission of the publisher.

To my parents
Hester and Brian Whitlock Blundell

τοῖς τεκοῦσι γὰρ
οὐδ' εἰ πονεῖ τις, δεῖ πόνου μνήμην ἔχειν.

Contents

Preface

This new translation of *Oedipus at Colonus* is aimed at all those, especially students and teachers, who wish to work with an English version that closely follows the Greek original. I have tried to remain reasonably faithful to Greek idiom and metaphor, to translate words important for the meaning of the play consistently, and, to a more limited extent, to retain the original word order, verse and sentence structure (though the meters have inevitably been sacrificed). This approach sometimes leads to awkward moments, but I hope they will be outweighed by its benefits. Though many aspects of the original have of course been lost, as they must be in any translation, I believe, and hope the reader will discover, that much of the poetry of meaning is best communicated in this way. Those who wish for a more mellifluous translation are already well served elsewhere.

The explanatory notes are aimed at those approaching this play, and perhaps all ancient Greek literature, for the first time. They provide factual information on such matters as mythology, geography and unfamiliar customs, together with clarification of obscure phrases and a few interpretive pointers. There are no stage directions in ancient Greek texts. Those provided in the translation are based on indications in the dialogue, and are designed to clarify the stage action for the modern reader. A fuller discussion of important background material concerning the poet, his theater, the myth of Oedipus and the religious context of the play is contained in the introduction. The translation is followed by an interpretive essay, to be read after the play, together with some suggestions for further reading.

I have generally followed A.C. Pearson's Oxford Classical Text (Oxford 1924), but have departed from it in a number of places. Pearson's colometry is reproduced, except in a few passages where I have increased the number of lines in order to avoid confusing the reader with inconsistent numbering. I regret that the new Oxford Classical Text, edited by Hugh Lloyd-Jones and Nigel Wilson, appeared too late for me to use it. My translation and notes are both indebted to Jebb's great work, which though dated is still unsurpassed.[1] Kamerbeek's more recent commentary has also been helpful for clarifying certain points. [2]

It gives me great pleasure to thank those who read and commented on an earlier draft of this work: Michael Halleran and James J. Clauss, my colleagues and the editors of this series, made many helpful criticisms; Michael Halleran also discussed a number of textual points with me, and kindly allowed me to use his diagram of the ancient theater; Ann Cumming made valuable suggestions for improving the introduction, and the translation benefited from her sharp eye for infelicities; Stephen Sharpe facilitated numerous hard decisions with his sound ear, patience and welcome common sense.

University of Washington
Seattle

---

1. R.C.Jebb, *Sophocles, the Plays and Fragments: Part II The Oedipus Coloneus* (3rd edition Cambridge 1900)
2. J.C. Kamerbeek, *The Plays of Sophocles: VII The Oedipus Coloneus* (Leiden 1984)

Introduction

Sophocles

Colonus, the rural village near Athens where *Oedipus at Colonus* is set, was the birthplace of Sophocles in about 495 BC. He was a generation younger than his great predecessor Aeschylus (c. 525-456), and ten or fifteen years older than Euripides (c. 480-406), the last of the three great Greek tragedians. The first dozen years of Sophocles' career thus overlapped with Aeschylus' final years, and for the rest of his long life Euripides was his rival. It is said that when Euripides died in 406 BC, Sophocles dressed his chorus in mourning at a public ceremony which preceded the dramatic festival. He himself was to die later the same year (or perhaps early in 405). In the fourth century and beyond, these three men rapidly became canonized as the three great figures of the Athenian tragic theater. This is the main reason why we still have some of their works, when the entire output of the other tragic playwrights has been lost. As with all ancient texts, the survival of these plays depended not only on the vagaries of taste, but on the chancy process of the copying and recopying of manuscripts until the advent of printing nearly two thousand years later.

Sophocles lived a long and active life, spanning almost the whole of the fifth century BC, which saw so many political and cultural achievements at Athens. We know almost nothing of his background (except that his father, Sophillus, is said to have owned a weapons factory), but the evidence of his career suggests a well-connected family. Like any Athenian boy whose father could afford it, he will have received the customary education in music, poetry and athletics. The mainstay of this education was Homer, especially the *Iliad*, which was thought to embody not just literary excellence but traditional cultural and moral values. As a boy, Sophocles will have learned to recite large chunks of the epic from memory. This must have been especially significant for the future playwright whom later writers were to describe as "most Homeric" of the tragedians.

The poet's childhood coincided with the Persian wars, in which the Greeks, largely under the leadership of Athens, repelled repeated Persian invasions of the Greek mainland. Sophocles was about five years old when the Athenians won their first great victory over the Persians at the battle of Marathon (490 BC). When the Persians were defeated again, in a sea-battle off the island of Salamis in 480 BC, the young Sophocles is said to have led the victory dance—a significant honor, as well as a tribute to the youth's good looks and physical grace. He grew to maturity in the years that followed the Persian wars, when the power and influence of Athens were on the rise. The city became the leader of the Delian League, an alliance of Greek states which was established after the wars for mutual defense, but which soon grew to resemble an Athenian empire rather than an alliance of free states. This period of Athenian history culminates in the leadership of Pericles, who was born around the same time as Sophocles and dominated public life from about 460 BC until his death in 429. He strengthened democracy at home and expanded Athenian influence abroad, in large part by exploiting Athenian leadership of the Delian League.

One of Pericles' most ambitious projects was the public building program which culminated in the construction of the Parthenon— the great temple of Athena on the acropolis at Athens. Like other such projects, this temple, with its magnificent architecture and sculptural decoration, was partly financed by taxes from members of the Delian League. Besides this kind of support for the visual arts, Pericles was a patron of writers and thinkers, helping to promote the extraordinary artistic and intellectual accomplishments of fifth-century Athens. Literary excellence was also fostered by the generally open and tolerant nature of the Athenian democratic ideal, which placed a high value on artistic achievement and freedom of expression. (It is worth remembering that Socrates was active as a provocative "gadfly" throughout most of this period, and was not prosecuted until 399 BC, after Athens had become demoralized by defeat and less tolerant of public criticism.)

But the cultural achievements of Periclean Athens meant little to the oppressed members of its empire or to its rivals, headed by Sparta. In 431 BC, when Sophocles was in his sixties, the resentment aroused by Athenian expansion culminated in the outbreak of the Peloponnesian war, between Athens with its allies on one side and Sparta with its allies on the other. This long and draining war dominated the last twenty-five years of the poet's life, and he was to die before it finally ended with the defeat of Athens in 404 BC.

Sophocles began his dramatic career in 468 BC with the lost *Triptolemus*, with which he defeated Aeschylus to win first prize. By this time tragedy in Athens had already developed into a mature and magnificent art form. But the conventions of tragedy were not static, and Sophocles had a reputation in antiquity as a theatrical innovator. Aristotle tells us in the *Poetics* that Sophocles increased the number of actors from two to three, and introduced the practice of scene painting. He is also said to have enlarged the size of the chorus from twelve to fifteen, written a book on dramaturgy and founded an artistic society dedicated to the Muses. In the course of his long career he wrote more than a hundred dramas—about 90 tragedies and 30 satyr plays (a kind of mythological burlesque). Of this enormous output we have only seven tragedies, significant parts of two satyr plays and some scattered fragments. We have secure production dates for only two of the surviving tragedies, which also happen to be the last of the seven: *Philoctetes*, produced in 409 BC, and *Oedipus at Colonus*, produced posthumously in 401 BC. *Antigone* may have been produced about 441 BC, and *Oedipus the King* somewhere between 430 and 425. The dating of the other extant tragedies—*Ajax*, *Electra* and *Women of Trachis*—is more speculative.

As was expected of male citizens of the leisured classes, Sophocles took an active part in the political, military and religious life of Athens. He served as public treasurer in 443/2 and was elected general at least once, in 440, when he served with Pericles. We are told that he was elected on the strength of the success of his play *Antigone* (which gives us a clue as to the date of that play). Though we may choose to doubt the truth of this story, it does suggest both the high regard in which a popular poet might be held, and the absence of any sharp dichotomy between achievement in artistic and political life. Whether or not this is how Sophocles got elected, however, a story about the military campaign helps bring him to life for us. When Pericles teased Sophocles as a mediocre strategist, he responded by displaying his strategic expertise in stealing a kiss from a handsome boy who was pouring the wine. Late in life Sophocles was again chosen for an important public office. In 413 BC Athens suffered a crushing defeat in Sicily, and the poet was one of ten commissioners appointed to reorganize Athenian affairs after the crisis. Another incident shows him participating in a different area of public life. In 420 BC the cult of Asclepius, god of medicine, was formally introduced into Athens. The god, who took the form of a snake, remained in the house of Sophocles until his official residence could be prepared. For this service the poet was honored after his death as a cult hero under the name of Dexion ("Receiver")[1].

Sophocles was probably acquainted with many of the most important cultural figures of his day. Besides the association with Pericles, his name is connected with such people as the philosopher Archelaus (the teacher of Socrates), and the historian Herodotus. *Oedipus at Colonus* itself provides evidence of his familiarity with Herodotus' work. When Oedipus compares his sons to the Egyptians, whose customs are said to be the opposite of the Greeks' (337-41), he is probably drawing on the colorful account in the second book of Herodotus' *Histories* (2.35). Sophocles also displays an unmistakable familiarity with the rhetorical techniques popularized by the contemporary thinkers known as sophists. These itinerant intellectuals offered instruction in many subjects, but especially rhetoric, which was the key to success in democratic politics. They found a ready audience at Athens, with its flourishing democracy, where public life was pervaded by debate. Public policy was decided by an assembly open to all male citizens, whose members voted on each issue after extensive debate. Athenian society was also highly litigious, and a citizen had to plead his own case in court before a jury of several hundred of his peers. It is therefore hardly surprising that the dramatists and their audience had a taste for this kind of rhetoric. Though Sophocles' style may seem less self-consciously rhetorical than that of Euripides, the influence of public debate can clearly be seen, for example in the long and formal speeches with which Oedipus and Creon answer each other's charges in *Oedipus at Colonus*.

Sophocles lived to the age of ninety, and several stories survive about his old age. One charming though wholly unreliable anecdote may be mentioned here. The story goes that in his old age the poet quarreled with his son Iophon, who then sued him for senility (the law allowed a son to take control of an incompetent father's

---

1. On hero cult see below, p. 12-14.

property). In his own defense, Sophocles read aloud in court from the play he was working on at the time: the opening of the song in praise of Attica from *Oedipus at Colonus* (668-73). Naturally he was acquitted.

Theater and performance

Greek tragedy was a peculiarly Athenian art form, and was closely bound up with the life of the city. It was enormously popular, in a way which may be hard to grasp today, drawing audiences of up to 15,000 from a citizen body of only about 100,000 men, women and children. There is no modern equivalent, for Athenian dramatic performances combined the status of a public institution with the broad popularity of a major Hollywood production and the artistic excellence of Shakespeare. The theater was so far from being an elitist form of entertainment that Pericles instituted a fund to enable poor citizens to buy tickets. The exact composition of the audience is, however, a matter of controversy. In particular it is not clear whether women were permitted to attend.

The Athenian theater also differed markedly from our own in that the plays were produced only once each, at public festivals in honor of Dionysus, god of wine and poetry. It was at his principal Athenian festival, the City Dionysia, that most of the great tragedians' works were first performed. This annual festival was an occasion for public festivity and civic pride, an opportunity for Athens to display itself and its cultural achievements to the world. It took place in the spring, when the sailing season had begun and visitors from all over the Greek world might be in town, including the members of the Delian league (who brought their tribute to Athens at this time of year, where it was displayed publicly in the theater). At the beginning of the festival a statue of Dionysus was carried in a torchlight procession to the theater, and it was present throughout the dramatic contest. But the plays were not religious rituals in any modern sense. Playwrights and performers were, of course, honoring the gods by their work, but the results were evaluated by artistic rather than religious criteria.

The tragedies at the City Dionysia were produced as part of a dramatic competition. Greek culture was highly competitive, and religious festivals often involved various kinds of contest—the Olympic games are a prominent example, and the City Dionysia included contests in comedy and choral song as well as tragedy. The tragic competition lasted for three days, with each of three poets producing three tragedies followed by one satyr play in the course of a single day. Sometimes the tragedies would constitute a connected trilogy, like Aeschylus' *Oresteia*, and even the satyr play might be on a related theme. But Sophocles seems to have preferred individual, self-contained dramas. The five judges who decided the contest were carefully selected by an elaborate procedure designed to ensure impartiality, and their decision was made under considerable pressure from a highly vocal crowd. Sophocles was exceptionally successful, winning at least eighteen victories and never coming third in the competition.

Since only three playwrights were allowed to put on their plays at each festival, even having one's plays produced was a competitive challenge. In keeping with the public nature of the event, a city official was in charge of "granting a chorus" to three finalists out of those who applied (how he reached his decision is unknown). A wealthy citizen was appointed to bear most of the production costs, as a kind of prestigious extra taxation. Chief among these costs was the considerable expense of training and costuming the chorus. The poet was his own producer, and originally acted as well, or employed professional actors (Sophocles is said to have been the first to stop acting in his own plays). But around the middle of the fifth century the state also assumed control of allocating the principal actor to each production, and began awarding a prize to the best actor.

The plays were performed in the open-air theater of Dionysus on the southern slope of the acropolis, which may have held as many as 15,000 people. In size and shape this huge theater resembled one end of a large football stadium (see diagram on p. 7). The judges sat in special seats at the front, along with the priests of Dionysus. Most of the audience probably sat on the ground, on the sloping sides of the acropolis hill above the theater. The performance area was dominated by a large round dancing floor, the *orchestra*, which was about seventy feet across. Behind it was a wooden stage-building, the *skene* (literally "tent" or "hut") which served as a set. Whether or not there was a raised stage in the fifth century is a matter of fierce controversy. If so, it was merely a low, narrow platform in front of the *skene*.[1] The stage-building usually represents a palace or other structure, but may also serve, for example, as a cave, or the grove that is the setting for *Oedipus at Colonus*. It had one or more doors through which characters could enter and exit, and was also used by the actors as a changing-room. Other entrances and exits, including those of the

---

1. For convenience, it is usual in discussing Greek drama to use the word "stage" to refer to the performance area, and I have followed that practice.

chorus, were made along the *parodoi*—two long ramps on either side of the *orchestra*. The same *parodos* is used consistently throughout the play to represent a particular destination. Thus in *Oedipus at Colonus* all visitors from Thebes will arrive from the same side, and those from Athens and Colonus from the other. It is dramatically effective for the two sides of the stage to represent Oedipus' friends and foes, while he remains at the center of the conflict. The length of the *parodoi* could also be exploited for dramatic purposes, as when Antigone excitedly watches the approach of Ismene (310-323).

In *Oedipus at Colonus* the *skene* represents the shrine of the Eumenides in the village of Colonus. To judge from Antigone's description (16-18), this was an impressive and picturesque spot.

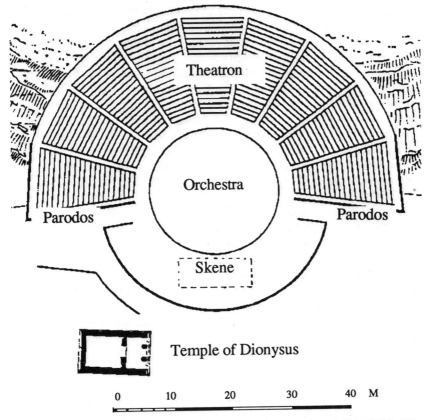

A reconstruction of the theater of Dionysus in Athens during the second half of the fifth century BC. (Based on the sketch by J. Travlos, *Pictorial Dictionary of Ancient Athens* [London 1971] 540.)

Bearing in mind Sophocles' supposed introduction of scene-painting (above, p. 3), it is plausible to suppose that the building was appropriately decorated. But the theater was so large that detailed scenery would not be easily visible to the audience. The grove was therefore probably indicated simply, leaving the imaginative appeal of poetic description to fill in the details. But however the *skene* was decorated, the action of the play requires a large rock, located in front of it but within the sacred area, for Oedipus to sit on (19). The low ledge further forward, where he sits later (192-6), may also have been part of the set, unless it was represented by the edge of the stage.

All the actors (including the chorus) were male. The sex, age and status of each character were indicated not only by costume but by masks covering the whole head. These masks were bold in design (as they had to be in order to be visible to spectators seated at the far edge of the theater), but naturalistic in manner. The lavish costumes included long, colorfully decorated robes, and sometimes tall (but thin-soled) boots. Details of costume would make clear the status of each character. A king like Theseus might carry a scepter, and old men like Oedipus and Creon would each have a staff.[1] Ismene is dressed for traveling, and wears a distinctive hat (313-4), and the costume of Oedipus and Antigone clearly indicates that they are beggars. As we learn from the shocked exclamations of Oedipus' visitors, his clothing is filthy and his hair unkempt, he carries a beggar's wallet, and the scars where he put out his eyes are plainly visible (see especially 551-6, 1256-63).

The standard number of speaking actors in a given production, apart from the chorus, was three, though there were usually several non-speaking extras playing silent parts such as guards and attendants. This explains why there are never more than three speaking characters on stage at one time, and accounts for some apparent peculiarities. Ismene, for example, is silent for nearly 500 lines from 1096 to 1555. After she exits through the grove at 509, the actor who plays her must return to play Theseus at 1096-1210, Polynices at 1249-1446 and Theseus again at 1500-1555. Meanwhile Ismene is played by a silent extra, until another actor is released by Oedipus' departure. As this example shows, the restriction to three speaking actors means that where, as in this play, there are more than three speaking characters, at least one actor would have to play more than one part. Moreover a single role often

---

1. Both these features are visible in the cover picture, which was probably influenced by this play.

had to be split between two or more actors. The latter practice is alien to the conventions of modern drama, but it was facilitated by the fact that the actors were all male, and wore not only distinctive costumes but rigid masks which identified each character clearly. Moreover the acting was highly stylized, and did not rely on subtle body movements or facial expressions (which were ruled out by the masks). Some Greek theaters have extraordinarily fine acoustics, but even so the actors must have delivered their lines loudly and emphatically, and used broad, clear gestures, in order to be seen and heard.

The fifteen-member chorus is sometimes important to the story (as in Aeschylus' *Eumenides*), but more usually represents a group of local citizens or other concerned persons. Though played by men, their characters are generally of the same sex as the central figure of the drama, with whom they enjoy a certain solidarity. In *Oedipus at Colonus* they are local citizens (1578) of noble birth (728), whose advanced age gives them a special sympathy with Oedipus (cf. 1239). The chorus members were masked and dressed in character like the main actors. At intervals throughout the drama, they performed a choral song, singing and dancing in unison. Although we know little about the choreography, it certainly included a strong mimetic element. The accompanying music, played on a double oboe-like instrument called an *aulos*, was simple and did not interfere with comprehension of the words, which are always significant for the drama and sometimes of the highest poetic complexity.

Chorus and actors were normally physically separated, performing in separate parts of the theater—the chorus in the *orchestra* and the actors in front of the *skene*. But the chorus-members are still characters in the drama. They have a single collective personality, as is shown by the fact that they speak and are addressed indiscriminately in the singular or plural. Sometimes they seem to participate quite vigorously in the stage action, for example in *Oedipus at Colonus* when they try to stop Creon from kidnapping Antigone (829-43). We do not know, however, how much actual physical contact took place between chorus and actors, or to what extent they moved into each other's performance areas. Moreover in most plays the chorus' effectiveness as a dramatic character is limited. In *Oedipus at Colonus*, for example, their age and frailty make their failure to prevent Antigone's abduction more plausible.

Greek tragedy is structured around the alternation of speech and song, which finds its visual counterpart in the two distinct

performance areas occupied by two different groups of partici-
pants. Most plays open with a spoken monologue or dialogue by
the actors (the prologue), which sets the scene and provides the
audience with any necessary background information. Sophocles
characteristically accomplishes this exposition through conversa-
tion rather than monologue. This opening scene is followed by the
arrival of the chorus, who enter singing the *parodos* or "entry song"
(not to be confused with the *parodos* or "entry ramp" by which they
arrive). They normally remain in the *orchestra* for the rest of the
play, performing further songs with dancing (known as *stasima* or
"songs in position") between the scenes of the drama, and participating to some extent in the action. This alternation of actors'
speech and choral song is a fluid form rather than a rigid structure.
Actors will sometimes shift into lyric meters, or converse with the
chorus in a sung dialogue, especially at moments of high emotion.
Such a dialogue may play the scene-dividing role of a choral ode,
or serve to vary the tone of a long scene. In *Oedipus at Colonus* the
chorus' entrance song (*parodos*) takes the unusual form of an
extended lyric dialogue between the chorus, Oedipus and Antigone
(117-253), and there are several subsequent passages of lyric
dialogue. Conversely the chorus leader (*coryphaeus*) not only leads
the dancing but exchanges a few spoken lines with the actors, as
the mouthpiece of the chorus as a whole.

A typical choral ode consists of a series of pairs of stanzas called
the "strophe" and "antistrophe." Each strophe has its own metrical
structure, which is repeated in the antistrophe. This strophic pair
is sometimes followed by an epode—an additional stanza with a
different metrical pattern (as at 1239-48). The meters of these lyric
passages are highly complex and varied. The actors' spoken lines,
by contrast, are in iambic trimeters, a regular six-beat meter that
approximates the rhythms of natural speech (rather like Shake-
spearean blank verse). The actors' speeches range in length from
the long rhetorical oration, or *rhesis*, to *stichomythia*, a formal kind
of dialogue in which the characters exchange single alternating
lines. Such modes of speech, like many other aspects of Greek
tragedy, may strike the modern audience as artificial. But every
kind of drama relies on its own formal conventions. We tend not to
notice the artificiality of our own theater (including film), because
familiarity makes its conventions seem natural to us.

Religion and Hero Cult

Oedipus at Colonus takes place in front of a sacred grove
containing a shrine to the goddesses known as Eumenides. There

is no evidence outside the play for such a shrine at Colonus at this period. But in view of the abundant geographical and religious detail throughout the work, much of which we know to be accurate, it would be most surprising if its central feature, the spot where the drama actually takes place, were not also familiar to the audience. The name Eumenides, or "Kindly Ones," is a euphemism, expressing a nervous desire for favor from goddesses who were in fact regarded with dread (similarly the Greek name for the dangerous Black Sea was "Hospitable Sea"). The chorus' reaction at the beginning of the play gives us some idea of the feelings these divinities inspired (125-32). Such awe stems from their sinister role as underworld goddesses of vengeance, in which aspect they are known as Erinyes or "Furies". As Erinyes they embody the justice of revenge, as we shall see in *Oedipus at Colonus*. They are especially associated with kin-murder, demanding blood for blood on behalf of the dead. This function is most memorably depicted in Aeschylus' *Eumenides*, where they appear as the play's chorus, mercilessly hounding Orestes for the murder of his mother. But Aeschylus' drama also presents them in a more positive light. At its conclusion they are installed in Athens as embodiments of fertility and divine blessing as well as the "dread," or respect for authority, that is essential to social order.

These ambivalent goddesses were worshipped under a variety of names in different places, as the stranger tells Oedipus (42-3). Besides "Kindly Ones" and "Furies," they are sometimes called "Curses" (Arai)—a title reflecting their role as the embodiment of vengeful curses, such as those that Oedipus calls down on his enemies (cf. 154, 864-5). In Thebes they were called "Ladies" (Potniai) (as Oedipus calls them at 84), while in Athens itself their cult name was "Solemn Ones" (Semnai) (note "solemn" at 41, 90, 101). Whatever name they go by, however, they are chthonian or earth powers, associated with death and the underworld, in contrast to the Olympians, the heavenly or sky gods (cf. 1654-5). This is clear not only from their function as avengers of the dead, but from their mythological parentage. In Hesiod they are children of Earth (*Theogony* 414), in Aeschylus of Night (*Eumenides* 416, 844), and in Sophocles of Earth and Darkness (40, 106). Their shrine at Athens, like that portrayed in the drama, was near a cavern believed to lead to the underworld. After making offerings to such gods one had to avert one's eyes (cf. 490), and the chorus tells us that it was customary to pass their shrine "without glancing, without speaking, without words" (130-31). A distinctive feature of their cult was the fact that they did not receive offerings of wine (cf. 100, 481).

Oedipus arrives at the shrine of these goddesses as a suppliant (44-5). Supplication was a ritual whereby anyone in trouble, especially a fugitive, might seek refuge and protection. One might supplicate someone personally by falling at his or her knees and touching the knees or chin in a ritual gesture. Alternatively one might supplicate at a sacred spot, such as a shrine or altar, as both Oedipus and Polynices do, and thus place the local inhabitants under an obligation to provide assistance. This obligation was enforced not only by the divinity at whose shrine the fugitive sought sanctuary, but by Zeus himself, protector of strangers and especially of suppliants. It is as suppliants that Oedipus and Antigone seek "honor" and "respect" from the people of Colonus (247, 286), as Polynices does later from his father (1268, 1273). Supplication is a common theme in legend, and many tragic plots are built around it. It provides a natural source of tension between fugitive, pursuer and rescuer, which makes it an ideal focus for dramatic action. But it was also an established practice in real life, made use of, for example, by criminals and political fugitives.

We know from evidence outside the play that Oedipus himself was an Athenian cult hero. "Hero" in this sense does not mean simply the principal character in a play or legend (though these legendary characters are often also cult heroes), but a great figure from the past who was honored with special rites after his death. The dead in general were regarded with great reverence in Greek society. Their surviving relatives made regular visits to their tombs, bringing offerings of food and drink and decorations such as wreaths, which were thought to bring honor and perhaps pleasure to the dead. The most common gifts were drink-offerings, of honey, milk, water, wine and olive oil, which would be poured onto the grave, or even into it through special feeding tubes. Such offerings were accompanied by prayers to the dead, who were begged to show benevolence towards their surviving relatives. Cult heroes, however, were in a special class, and had a public significance extending beyond their immediate family. Unlike the ordinary dead, they were regularly honored with animal sacrifice as well as drink-offerings and other gifts, and their tombs were treated as shrines. They were believed to have—and to use freely— exceptional powers to help or harm their living friends and foes from beyond the grave. They thus enshrined the essence of traditional Greek morality, which was based on reciprocal help between friends and harm between enemies.

Since they lie buried in the earth, cult heroes are, like the Eumenides, chthonian or "earth" powers, in contrast to the "sky" gods or Olympians. They have a strongly local significance for the region where they are buried. If properly appeased they may bring the community fertility, prosperity and above all help in battle. Theseus allegedly appeared and helped the Athenians win the battle of Marathon, and Ajax assisted at the battle of Salamis (the island of his birth), while the Locrians used to leave a gap in the battle line for their local hero to defend. In order to gain these advantages, the actual presence of the hero's body was of great importance. The Athenians brought home the bones of Theseus, and the Spartans those of Orestes, in the latter case specifically to ensure a military victory. This explains the importance attached in *Oedipus at Colonus* to the location of Oedipus' grave. Although he has physically disappeared, it clear that he is to be thought of as remaining somehow present in Athenian soil (cf. especially 621-2). Despite his age and feebleness in life, his grave will bring Athens military victory over Thebes.

In keeping with their role as military defenders, the tombs of heroes were strategically placed. Unlike ordinary graves, which were located outside the city walls, theirs might be within the city, or built into the city-wall, or placed inside a religious sanctuary. All these special locations are appropriate to their role as guardians of the city. Such practices are reflected in *Oedipus at Colonus*, in Oedipus' disappearance at a sacred spot which is well placed for defending Athens from invaders. The Thebans likewise hope to win such benefits by placing him just outside Theban territory (399-405). This plan is a naive one, however, for it neglects the fact that in addition to a hero's body, his good will must be secured (cf. 402-3). Otherwise he may strike the land with plague, barrenness or war.

Heroic status was by no means confined to virtuous or benevolent figures. Some bizarre and even criminal characters received such honors after their death. At Astypalaea a boxer killed his opponent in a match, went berserk and destroyed a school full of sixty children, and yet was honored after his death as a hero. The only thing all heroes have in common is that they are mighty figures of special local significance, for better or worse. "It is some extraordinary quality that makes the hero; something unpredictable and uncanny is left behind and is always present."[1] Despite this quality, however, and despite their supernatural powers, cult

---

1. W. Burkert, *Greek Religion* (Eng. trans. Cambridge, Mass. 1985) 208.

heroes remain clearly distinct from the gods proper. They are dead mortals with special powers, rather than immortal gods. Unlike the gods, their sphere of influence is confined to the immediate vicinity of their tomb. And although many cult heroes are legendary characters, ordinary mortals continued to be promoted to their ranks. Solon's tomb in Salamis was thought to protect the island, and Sophocles himself was made a cult hero after his death (above, p. 4).

In the course of *Oedipus at Colonus* we see Oedipus transformed from a helpless, blind old beggar into an awe-inspiring figure, with uncanny powers for good and ill, who meets a miraculous death. The play thus dramatizes the process of "heroization," and this makes it a unique document. In particular, Oedipus' mysterious disappearance through the direct intervention of the gods is unparalleled. It is the climax of the special destiny the gods have promised him, which enables him, despite the taint of his terrible past, to call himself "sacred" and "reverent" (287). This sacred status gives him an extraordinary right to intrude into the forbidden grove of the Eumenides, with whom his cult as a hero was historically associated. There was a shrine to Oedipus himself at Colonus, and a tomb of Oedipus in the shrine of the "Solemn Ones" (Semnai) at Athens (no doubt reflecting a rival tradition about his death). So too in Sophocles' play, he enjoys a special kinship with these goddesses,[1] and becomes the willing agent of their power to bless and curse.

The Myth

Oedipus is most familiar to the modern mind as the hero of Sophocles' *Oedipus the King*, who falls from the pinnacle of human accomplishment to the depths of an excruciating self-awareness, blinding himself when he discovers that he has unwittingly killed his father, Laius, and married his own mother, Jocasta. He has become a universal symbol not only of the tragic blindness of the human condition, but also, thanks to the incalculable influence of Freud, of the deepest and most terrible fears and desires of the unconscious. The earliest myth of Oedipus, however, makes him no such figure of doom. In the *Odyssey* we hear that, though he was distressed at the discovery of his deeds, he went on ruling at Thebes (11.271-80). There is no mention of his self-blinding, though his mother/wife hanged herself, leaving him to suffer from her Erinyes (avenging spirits or furies). The *Iliad* mentions that

---

1. See further Interpretation p. 92.

he died violently—perhaps in battle or a fight—and was honored at Thebes with funeral games (23.679-80). Various lost epics recounted his story in greater detail. In one fragment we hear that he cursed his sons while still at Thebes, because they set on his table the wine-cups of Laius (thus presumably reminding him of his parricide). The Erinys heard his curse that his sons should be at strife forever.[1] The Erinys also appears in a poem of Pindar (*Olympian* 2.35-9), causing the sons' mutual fratricide as a direct consequence of Oedipus' parricide. In Aeschylus' lost version, when Oedipus discovered the truth he both blinded himself and cursed his sons.

Oedipus the King, probably produced some time between 430 and 425 BC, opens upon Oedipus as the King of Thebes, beloved by his people, an intelligent, confident and compassionate man in the prime of life. He was raised in Corinth, but left that city in an attempt to evade a prophecy from Apollo's oracle at Delphi that he was to murder his father and marry his mother.[2] Before reaching Thebes he was provoked by an unknown man at a crossroads, and killed him. Travelling on to Thebes, he found the city terrorized by the sphinx, a winged monster with a woman's head and a lion's body, who killed anyone who could not answer her riddle. Oedipus solved the riddle and saved the city. In gratitude, the Thebans gave him the crown of their recently murdered king, Laius, and the hand of the queen in marriage. In the course of Sophocles' drama Oedipus discovers that he is actually the son of Laius, who was the unknown man at the crossroads, and Jocasta, who is now his own wife. Although this aspect of the story is not emphasized in Sophocles' treatment, Oedipus has inherited the malignant doom that fell upon the house of Laius, who (at least according to some versions of the myth) offended the gods and was warned by Apollo not to have any children. (This is mentioned, for example, by Aeschylus, *Seven Against Thebes* 742-52.) When *Oedipus at Colonus* alludes to the doom or curse that lies over the house of Oedipus (e.g. 369, 596, 965), this may be traced back not only to Oedipus' own deeds, but to those of his father before him.

When Sophocles' Oedipus discovers the dreadful truth, he puts out his own eyes in horror and longs only to go into exile from Thebes. Since he acted in ignorance and (in the case of the parricide) in self-defence, he would be found innocent in a court of law

---

1. Erinys is the singular of Erinyes. "The Erinys" means the avenging spirit of this particular deed or family.
2. Thebes, Corinth and Delphi are identified on the map of mainland Greece (below, p. 88.)

(ancient as well as modern). But guilt and innocence have little to do with the kind of horror aroused by such revelations. Despite his moral innocence, Oedipus is a polluted man—a tainted outcast who risks bringing divine retribution not only on himself, but on all who associate with him. At the end of the play his fate is left uncertain. He is dependent on Creon, his brother-in-law and successor as king, who will not allow him to go into exile without first consulting the Delphic oracle.

Some twenty years after the first production of this play, Sophocles, by now an old man himself, returned to complete the story of Oedipus. The dramatic movement of the later play is the reverse of Oedipus' fall from greatness in *Oedipus the King*. This time he starts out at the nadir of his fortunes, and grows into a figure of heroic stature. When the play opens, a large but unspecified number of years has passed since the events dramatized in *Oedipus the King*. At the end of the earlier play, Oedipus' offspring appear on the stage as children. By the time of his expulsion some time later, the boys were apparently old enough to speak up on his behalf (427-30), and Antigone to become his guide and companion. But although Oedipus himself is an old man in *Oedipus at Colonus*, his daughters are portrayed as still young girls. At the same time Creon tactlessly implies (751-2) that Antigone is rather beyond the proper age for marriage (about fifteen for girls in ancient Greece). We should not try too hard, however, to reconcile the ages of the characters in the two plays. More significant is the emphasis on the many years that Oedipus has wandered, and on his old age, the effects of which have been enhanced by his terrible sufferings, in contrast to the youthfulness of his children.

Throughout *Oedipus at Colonus* the events of *Oedipus the King* are recalled, especially in Oedipus' reiterated self-defense for the terrible deeds of his past (265-74, 521-48, 960-1002). At the end of the play Sophocles alludes to another part of the myth, which he himself had dramatized in his play *Antigone*, produced even earlier than *Oedipus the King*.[1] Antigone's promise that she will return to Thebes and bury Polynices (1405-13, 1435-6, 1769-72) points forward in legendary time to the plot of the play that bears her name. These three tragedies, often called Sophocles "Theban plays," thus focus on the same family and the terrible events that befall it. They are not, however, a trilogy. Unlike the three plays of Aeschylus' *Oresteia*, they were written at wide intervals, without following the legendary order of events. Each is a dramatic unity, and they

---

1. On the dating of the plays see above, p. 3.

were never intended to be performed together. Nevertheless, the allusions in *Oedipus at Colonus* show Sophocles had not forgotten, and perhaps hoped that his audience would remember, the thematic threads that connect this play with his other Theban dramas.

Though the tragedians nearly always worked with the traditional tales, whose broad outlines were familiar to their audience, they were free to vary the legendary details for their own dramatic purposes. Accordingly Sophocles introduces a number of apparent innovations in his treatment of the myth of Oedipus and his sons. One small but interesting variation from other versions known to us is that Polynices is the elder son (374-6, 1292-8, 1422-3). Euripides makes him younger than Eteocles, and no one but Sophocles makes either brother's claim to the throne depend on primogeniture. Instead the two brothers are usually said to have agreed to rule alternately. Eteocles is first, but refuses to surrender the throne at the end of his allotted time, giving Polynices a legitimate grievance against him. Since primogeniture was not a Greek custom, Sophocles' innovation means that Polynices is less obviously justified in his resentment, or at least that the audience is likely to have had less sympathy for his case. It also gives Oedipus an additional reproach to hurl against the son who appears before him, for as the first to rule he was also the first who might have recalled his father (cf. 1354-9). Sophocles has adapted a detail of the myth to prevent us from choosing sides between the brothers. Both are equally guilty, and equally damned.

Another variation in Sophocles' treatment of the myth is more substantial. In earlier accounts known to us, Oedipus' curse upon his sons is delivered at Thebes, and is the cause of the strife between them. In *Oedipus at Colonus*, however, the curse occurs years later, and is itself a consequence of the brothers' strife. This enables the poet to exploit Oedipus' curse for maximum dramatic impact within his play. It also makes the curse more justifiable, since Oedipus does not utter it until his sons have come to blows, after already neglecting him for many years. Yet Polynices seems to know already about his father's avenging spirit or Erinys (1298-9), and Oedipus himself mentions earlier curses (1375). Though the latter could simply refer to his previous imprecations within the play (421-7), it is certainly not difficult to imagine Oedipus cursing his sons repeatedly over the years. But we need not insist on perfect clarity. The important point for the drama is that the curse we witness is the decisive one, uttered as Oedipus is rapidly acquiring the cult hero's superhuman powers.

Oedipus at Colonus

CHARACTERS

OEDIPUS, former king of Thebes
ANTIGONE, daughter of Oedipus
STRANGER, a resident of Colonus
CHORUS, fifteen aged noblemen of Colonus
ISMENE, daughter of Oedipus
THESEUS, king of Athens
CREON, Oedipus' brother-in-law, king of Thebes
POLYNICES, son of Oedipus
MESSENGER, an attendant of Theseus
Guards and **attendants** of Theseus, Creon's armed **escort**

Setting: A grove sacred to the goddesses called Eumenides ("Kindly Ones")[1] *at Colonus, a rural village near Athens.*[2] *Within the sacred precinct is a large rock, which forms a seat, and an opening through which one may exit into the grove at the rear. Just outside the precinct is a low ledge of natural rock.*

(Enter Oedipus, who is old and blind, guided by his young daughter Antigone. They are dressed as beggars, and Oedipus carries a staff and

---

1. On the Eumenides see Introduction p. 10-11.
2. The Greek *polis* or city state included not just the city proper, but the rural lands and villages surrounding it, which in the case of Athens make up the territory known as Attica. Colonus (Sophocles' birthplace) was about a mile and a quarter north-west of Athens (see map of Attica below, p. 83). It was politically part of Athens, and its people were Athenian citizens.

a beggar's pouch. They enter along one of the parodoi *or entrance ramps, which throughout the play will represent the road from Thebes.)*

OEDIPUS:
Antigone, child of this blind old man,[3] to what
region have we come, or what men's city?
Who will welcome Oedipus the wanderer
this day, with scanty gift-giving?
I beg little, but obtain still less   5
than little—yet that suffices me.
For my sufferings and time, my long companion,
and thirdly my nobility, teach me to acquiesce.
But child, if you see anywhere to sit,
either in a public place or in a grove of the gods,   10
stop me and settle me there, so that we can inquire
where we are. For as strangers we need to learn
from citizens and fulfill whatever we are told.

ANTIGONE:
Father, long-suffering Oedipus, the towers that
shield the city are, to judge by eye, far off.[4]   15
But this place is sacred, one may clearly surmise, luxuriant
with laurel, olive and vine. A throng of feathered
nightingales sing their blessed song within it.[5]
Rest your limbs, then, and sit on this rough rock.
For you have traveled a long road for an old man.   20

OEDIPUS:
Seat me, then, and guard me in my blindness.

ANTIGONE:
After so much time I don't need to learn that.

(She seats him on the large rock within the sacred precinct.)

OEDIPUS:
Can you tell me where we have arrived?

ANTIGONE:
I know we are at Athens, but I do not know this place.

OEDIPUS:
Yes, every traveler told us that much at least.   25

ANTIGONE:
Shall I go off and learn what this spot is?

---

3. Oedipus blinded himself out of horror when he discovered that he had unwittingly murdered his father and married his mother. These events are dramatized in Sophocles' earlier play, *Oedipus the King* (see Introduction p. 14-16).

4. The most prominent feature of these "towers" was the Athenian acropolis, which rose up behind the spectators in the theater of Dionysus.

5. It has been pointed out that nightingales arrive in Greece at about the same time as the spring festival of Dionysus, when the play was first performed.

OEDIPUS:
Yes, child, if indeed it is habitable.

ANTIGONE:
It is certainly inhabited.

(Enter a local stranger along the other parodos, *which represents the road from the adjacent village of Colonus and from Athens.)*
But I don't think there is
any need; for I see a man here near to us.

OEDIPUS:
Is he moving forward and proceeding this way?   30

ANTIGONE:
No, he is present now. Whatever you may
opportunely say, declare it, for the man is here.

OEDIPUS:
Stranger, hearing from this girl, who sees on my behalf
as well as her own, that you have come to us as an auspicious
informant, to tell us what is not plain to us...   35

STRANGER:
Before asking the rest, get away from that seat!
For you occupy a place not pure to tread upon.

OEDIPUS:
What is this place? To which of the gods is it held sacred?

STRANGER:
Untouchable and uninhabitable! For the fearful goddesses
occupy it, daughters of Earth and Darkness.[6]   40

OEDIPUS:
By what solemn name, when I hear it, should I pray to them?

STRANGER:
People here would call them the all-seeing Eumenides.
But elsewhere other names are considered fine.

OEDIPUS:
Then may they welcome graciously their suppliant,[7]
for never again shall I leave my seat in this land.   45

STRANGER:
What is this?

OEDIPUS:
It is the watchword of my fate.[8]

---

6. On the parentage and various names of the Eumenides see Introduction p. 11.
7. On supplication see Introduction p. 11-12.
8. This phrase is as mysterious in Greek as in English. We shall shortly discover that Apollo's oracle prophesied rest and death for Oedipus at a shrine of the "solemn goddesses" (84-93). So when Oedipus hears to whom the grove is sacred, he recognizes it as the "watchword," established by Apollo, which marks the end of his sufferings.

STRANGER:
Well, I have not the confidence to expel you without word
from the city, before informing them what you are doing.

OEDIPUS:
By the gods now, stranger, do not dishonor me,
vagrant that I am, by failing to answer my entreaty.   50

STRANGER:
Reveal your question, and I at least shall not dishonor you.

OEDIPUS:
What then is this place that we have stepped into?

STRANGER:
You shall hear and understand all I know of it myself.
This whole place is sacred. Solemn Poseidon
occupies it,[9] and the fire-bearing god is within,   55
the Titan Prometheus.[10] But the spot that you are trampling
is called the bronze-stepped threshold of this land,
the mainstay of Athens.[11] The nearby fields
proclaim this horseman here, Colonus, as their
founder.[12] All the people have been named   60
after this man, and bear his name in common.
Such is this area, stranger, honored
not in legend but more highly, by our company.

OEDIPUS:
So people dwell here in this region?

STRANGER:
Most certainly, taking their name from this god here.   65

OEDIPUS:
Does anyone rule them, or is speech with the people?[13]

---

9. Poseidon, god of the sea and of horses, had an altar at Colonus. It is not
part of the set, but provides a convenient off-stage location for Theseus,
who must remain available for quick entrances (cf. 887-9, 1491-5).

10. Prometheus was the son of the Titan Iapetos. He stole fire from the gods
to give to mortals, and was represented in art as carrying a torch.

11. The place is named after a nearby spot (not represented on stage),
probably a cave or fissure in the earth, believed to be an entrance (hence
"threshold") to the underworld. This is where Oedipus will finally meet
his end (1590-91). It is the "mainstay" of Athens both because it represents
the ancient earth on which the city stands, and because it is a sacred spot
providing religious protection.

12. Colonus was the eponymous founding hero of the region. The stranger
points in the direction of his statue, either on or (more likely) off the stage.
Such heroes might receive divine honors (hence "god" in 65). On hero-cult
in general see Introduction p. 12-14.

13. Oedipus is asking whether the government is a monarchy or a democracy.

STRANGER:
This area is ruled by the king in the city.
OEDIPUS:
Who is this man, holding power in speech and strength?
STRANGER:
He is called Theseus, offspring of Aegeus before him.
OEDIPUS:
Could one of you go to him as an envoy?   70
STRANGER:
For what purpose? To speak to him, or prepare him to come?
OEDIPUS:
So that by giving a little aid he may win great profit.
STRANGER:
What aid can come from a sightless man?
OEDIPUS:
The words I have to say will all be seeing.[14]
STRANGER:
You know, stranger—do not slip up now. For you are   75
noble, as far as one can see, but for your fate.[15]
Remain here, where you appeared, until I
go and tell this to the local people—those living here,
not in the city. For they will decide
whether you must stay or travel on again.   80

(Exit stranger along the parodos *by which he entered.)*
OEDIPUS:
Child, has the stranger gone from us?
ANTIGONE:
He's gone. You can say anything
in peace, father, for I alone am near.

(Oedipus raises his hands in prayer to the Eumenides.)
OEDIPUS:
Dread-eyed ladies, since it is at your seat that I
have now first rested my limbs within this land,   85

---

14. This mysterious phrase echoes the description of the Eumenides as "all-seeing" (42). The blind were thought especially capable of prophecy and divine inspiration, a power of mental "vision" compensating for their physical blindness. Thus Oedipus' words will display the power of sight that his eyes lack.
15. "Fate" here, and at 1337, 1370, 1443 and 1750, translates the Greek word *daimon*, literally "divinity." Since disasters as well as blessings come from the gods, this word can be used for bad or good fortune, and is used here by the stranger for Oedipus' manifest blindness and poverty. The word translated "fate" at 46, 255, 596, 963, 1014 and 1470 (*sumphora*) also refers to good or bad fortune, especially the latter. Neither these nor other words translated as "fate" or "destiny" imply predestination.

be not unfeeling towards myself or Phoebus,[16]
who, when he prophesied to me those many evils,
said that this, in the length of time, would be my rest:
that when I came at last to a country where I might find
the seat and hospitality of solemn goddesses,   90
there I would round the post of my long-suffering life,[17]
bringing profit by residing there to those who welcomed me,
but doom to those who sent me away, driving me out.
He pledged to me that signs would come of these events—
an earthquake, or perhaps thunder, or a flash from Zeus.[18]   95
I recognize now that it was certainly
a trusty omen from you that guided me
along this road to this grove. For never otherwise
would I have met you first as I journeyed—
I sober and you wineless[19]—nor would I have sat   100
upon this solemn unhewn step. But, goddesses,
in accordance with the voice of Apollo, grant me
now some closure and conclusion of my life—
unless I seem somehow to fall short, being forever
enslaved to the most extreme toils of any mortal.   105
Come, sweet daughters of ancient Darkness!
Come Athens, called the city of greatest
Pallas,[20] most honored of all cities!
Take pity on this miserable shade of Oedipus
the man—for his body is not that of long ago.   110

ANTIGONE:
Silence! For here are some people, aged by time,
approaching to spy out your seat.

OEDIPUS:
I shall be silent. And you, conceal me away
from the road, in the grove, until I can learn
what they will say. For in learning   115
lies the safeguard of the things we do.

---

16. Phoebus ("Bright") was a common name for Apollo, god of music and
    prophecy, who was sometimes identified with Helios, god of the sun. It
    was his oracle at Delphi that prophesied Oedipus' terrible fate in *Oedipus
    the King* (see Introduction p. 15).
17. The metaphor refers to the turning point in a chariot race, after which
    the contestants headed for the finishing line.
18. Zeus, king of the gods and lord of the sky, was the sender of thunder
    and lightning.
19. Unlike most Greek divinities, the Eumenides never received wine as
    an offering (cf. 481). Oedipus is called "sober" because of the austerity of
    his recent life, but the word also suggests the special affinity that unites
    him to the goddesses (see Interpretation p. 92).
20. Pallas is a frequent name for Athena, patron goddess of Athens.

(Exeunt Oedipus and Antigone into the grove. Enter the chorus of fifteen aged noblemen of Colonus, singing and dancing, along the parodos *representing the road from Colonus, and into the orchestra.)*[21]

Strophe A

CHORUS:
Look! Who was it, then?
Where is he dwelling?
Where has he sped to away from here, of all,
all people most outrageous?   120
Glance about! Look for him!
Search about everywhere!
A wanderer,
the old man is some wanderer, and not
from these parts. For otherwise he would never   125
have stepped into the untrodden grove
of these unconquerable maidens,
whose name we tremble to say,
whom we pass by
without glancing,   130
without speaking, without words,
moving silent lips to express our reverent thought.
But now there is word that one
has come who shows no awe;
and I, looking round the whole   135
precinct, cannot yet
perceive where he is dwelling.[22]

(Enter Oedipus and Antigone from the grove. They converse with the chorus in song.[23]*)*

OEDIPUS:
I am that man! For I can see you by your voices,
as the saying goes.

CHORUS:
Oh! Oh!   140
Dreadful to see! Dreadful to hear!

OEDIPUS:
Do not, I supplicate, look on me as lawless.

---

21. The chorus' entrance song (*parodos*) takes the unusual form of a lengthy lyric dialogue between the chorus, Oedipus and Antigone (117-253). Like most songs in tragedy, it consists of a series of metrically equivalent pairs of stanzas, each pair consisting of a strophe and answering antistrophe. But here the structure is complex and somewhat irregular.

22. Note that the chorus refer to themselves indiscriminately as "I" or "we." This alternation is quite usual, and reflects that fact that their character is a collective one.

23. When characters other than the chorus use song, the effect is usually one of heightened emotion.

CHORUS:
Zeus the Protector, whoever is the old man?

OEDIPUS:
One by no means to be called blessed
for his preeminent fate, guardians of this country.   145
But that is plain. For otherwise I would not
be moving thus with the help of another's eyes,
or be anchored, great as I am, upon the small.

Antistrophe A

CHORUS:
Ah! Ah!
Your sightless eyes,   150
were they thus from birth? Your life has been wretched,
and lengthy too, one may surmise.
But you shall not, if I can help it,
bring down these further curses.
For you are transgressing,   155
transgressing! But—lest you intrude
within this grassy voiceless
glade, where a bowl of water
runs together with a flow
of honeyed drink-offerings   160
(take good care to avoid
these things, ill-fated stranger)—
move away, step back!
A long path bars you from us—
do you hear, much-toiling vagrant?   165
If you have any word to offer
for discussion with me,
step back from where no one may step,
and where it is lawful for all to do so,
speak; but until then, refrain.

OEDIPUS:
Daughter, to what counsel should we turn?   170

ANTIGONE:
Father, the citizens' concerns must be ours likewise,
yielding and listening as need be.

OEDIPUS:
Then place your hand on me.

ANTIGONE:
　　　　　　　　　　I'm touching you now.

OEDIPUS:
Strangers, let me indeed suffer no injustice,
if I trust you and move away.   175

Strophe B

CHORUS:
Never, old man, be sure,
shall anyone take you
from these seats against your will.[24]

(Guided by Antigone, Oedipus moves forward a short distance.)

OEDIPUS:
Further, then?

CHORUS:
                          Step further forward.

(They move forward a little more.)

OEDIPUS:
Further?

CHORUS:
                          Lead him on, girl—   180
forward. For you understand.

ANTIGONE:
Come, keep following. Follow this way on your blind
feet, father, where I lead you.[25]

CHORUS:
Endure, as a stranger in a strange land,
enduring man, to loath   185
whatever the city does not hold dear,
and to revere what is dear to it.

OEDIPUS:
Then take me, child,
to a place where, entering on reverence,[26]
we may both speak and listen.   190
Let us not war against necessity.

(Antigone leads her father outside the sacred precinct to a natural ledge of rock, which is big enough to serve as a low seat, but is distinct from the larger rock within the sacred area where Oedipus sat earlier.)

Antistrophe B

CHORUS:
There! Direct your feet no further away
from that ledge of natural rock.

OEDIPUS:
Like this?

---

24. The chorus are emphatically guaranteeing that Oedipus may remain safely in the vicinity of the grove, with its rocky "seats," even after he has left the sacred area which includes the rock where he was sitting earlier.

25. A few lines may be missing from the text at about this point, but editors disagree over precisely where, if anywhere, the lacuna falls.

26. I.e. entering an area where it is not impious to tread.

CHORUS:
>That's enough, as you can hear.

OEDIPUS:
Shall I sit down?

CHORUS:
>Yes, turn and sit on the front   195
of the stony ledge, crouching down low.

ANTIGONE:
Father, this is my task. Peacefully...

OEDIPUS:
Oh alas! Alas!

ANTIGONE:
... fit step to step,
leaning your aged body   200
on my friendly arm.

OEDIPUS:
Alas for my malignant doom!

(Antigone settles her father on his new seat.)

CHORUS:
Enduring man, now that you are comfortable,
tell us, what mortal are you by birth?
Who are you, led along in such pain? What   205
fatherland might I discover to be yours?

OEDIPUS:
Strangers, I am citiless. But don't...

CHORUS:
What's this you are prohibiting, old man?

OEDIPUS:
Don't! Don't! Don't ask me
who I am! Don't probe   210
by seeking further!

CHORUS:
What's this?

OEDIPUS:
>Dread is my birth!

CHORUS:
>   Tell!

OEDIPUS:
Child—alas!—what am I to say?

CHORUS:
Of what seed are you—speak,
stranger!—on your father's side?   215

OEDIPUS:
Alas, what am I to suffer, my child?

ANTIGONE:
Speak, for you are stepping towards the brink.

OEDIPUS:
Then I shall speak, for I have no way to hide it.

CHORUS:
You two are making long delays. Now be quick!

OEDIPUS:
Do you know one born from Laius?[27]

CHORUS:
                    Oh!   220

OEDIPUS:
And the family of the Labdacids?[28]

CHORUS:
               Oh Zeus!

OEDIPUS:
The miserable Oedipus?

CHORUS:
            What? Are *you* that man?

OEDIPUS:
Have no dread at what I say!

CHORUS:
Oh! Oh! Oh!

OEDIPUS:
       Ill-fated am I!

CHORUS:
           Oh! Oh!

OEDIPUS:
Daughter, what will happen now?   225

CHORUS:
Out! Go far from this country!

OEDIPUS:
But how will you redeem the promises you made?

CHORUS:
Fated payment comes to no one
for repaying what he suffered first.[29]
One deceit matched to other   230
deceits gives pain, not favor,
to have in return.

---

27. Laius was Oedipus' father, whom he killed in ignorance of their relationship (see Introduction p. 15). His descendants are called the Labdacids.
28. Labdacus was Laius' father. His descendants are called the Labdacids.
29. I.e. one is justified in injuring someone who has first injured oneself. The language of payment and repayment is often used in Greek to express the idea of retaliatory justice (e.g. 994-5) or, conversely, reciprocal favors and friendship (e.g. 635, 1203).

Away again from these seats![30]
Set out from my land once more in haste,
lest you attach some further   235
debt to my city![31]

(The parodos *ends, and the meter returns to the iambic trimeters used
for spoken dialogue.)*

ANTIGONE:
Respectful-minded strangers,[32]
since you could not endure
my old father here—having heard
tell of his unwilling deeds[33]—   240
at least, I supplicate you, strangers,
pity my wretched self. For I
beseech you on behalf of my father alone—
beseech you, looking into your eyes
with eyes that are not blind, like one born   245
from your own blood—that the miserable man
may meet respect. For on you as on a god
we who have endured depend. Come now, grant
this unexpected favor, I beseech you
by whatever you have that is dear to you—   250
child, marriage-bed, property, or god.
For if you searched you would not see a mortal who,
if a god leads him on, could escape.[34]

CHORUS LEADER:
Know, child of Oedipus, that we pity
both you and this man likewise for your fate.   255
But, trembling at what comes from the gods, we lack the strength

---

30. The verbal echo of 178 emphasizes the fact that the chorus are
breaking their promise.
31. The chorus fear that Oedipus' polluting presence will force them to
"pay" a "debt" of suffering to the gods. On pollution see Introduction p.
15-16.
32. "Respect" (*aidos*) is an important concept in popular Greek ethics. It
implies a sensitivity to the due claims of others, whether divine or mortal.
Antigone refers here to the chorus' religious reasons for rejecting Oedipus. But she will also beg for the "respect" due to suppliants (247), as
Polynices does later (1268).
33. Oedipus' past deeds are described here and elsewhere as "unwilling"
or performed "against his will" (e.g. 522, 964, 977, 987), for although he
willingly killed Laius and married Jocasta, he was ignorant at the time
of their relationship to himself, and therefore did not "willingly" murder
his father or marry his mother.
34. The gods were traditionally thought to lead into trouble those mortals
whom they wished to destroy. In Oedipus' case, the god is Apollo, whose
oracle prophesied his terrible deeds (see Introduction p. 15).

to say more than what has now been said to you.

OEDIPUS:
What use is glory then? What use is
fine reputation flowing away in vain?
For people say that Athens is most reverent, 260
that it alone can save the maltreated stranger,
that it alone is able to give him aid.
For *me* where are those claims? After raising me up
from these steps of rock you are driving me out,
dreading nothing but my name—certainly not 265
my body or my deeds; for my deeds at least
were suffered rather than perpetrated
(if it were right to tell the tale of my mother and father,
for which you fear me so)—that I well
know. Yet in my nature how am I evil? 270
I acted in return for what I suffered, so that if I had done it
with understanding, not even then would I have been evil.
But as it was, I reached the point I reached knowing nothing,
while those from whom I suffered tried knowingly to kill me.[35]

    Therefore I supplicate you, strangers, by the gods, 275
just as you made me move away, so also save me,
and by no means, while honoring the gods, deny the gods
their due. You should consider that
they look upon the reverent among mortals,
they look upon the irreverent, nor has escape 280
yet come to any impious mortal man.
With their help, then, do not cloud the blessedness
of Athens by ministering to impious deeds.
But, just as you took the suppliant under pledge,
rescue and guard me fully. And do not, seeing 285
this face so hard to look upon, dishonor me.
For I have come here sacred, reverent, and bringing
benefit to these citizens. When whoever has
authority is here, the man who is your leader,
then you shall hear and understand all. But 290
in the meantime, by no means behave evilly.

CHORUS LEADER:
There is great necessity, old man, to stand in awe
of the reasons you give; for they have been expressed
in no slight words. But it suffices for me
that the lords of the land should decide this matter. 295

OEDIPUS:
And where, strangers, is he who governs this country?

CHORUS LEADER:
At his father's city in this land. But an informant,

---

35. Oedipus' parents attempted to destroy him as a baby, in order to avoid
    Apollo's prophecies.

who also sent me here, has gone to summon him.

OEDIPUS:
Do you think he will have any consideration or thought
for the blind man, to bring him here in person?   300

CHORUS LEADER:
Most certainly, when once he hears your name.

OEDIPUS:
But who is there to report that word to him?

CHORUS LEADER:
The path is long, but numerous travelers' tales
love to wander abroad. Hearing them, he will
be here—have confidence! For your name, old man,   305
has spread greatly among all, so that even if he is slow
with sleep, hearing of you he will arrive here quickly.

OEDIPUS:
Then may he arrive with good fortune both for his own city
and for me! For what good man is not his own friend?

*(Antigone catches sight of a figure in the distance, not yet visible to the
audience. Her excited speech is in iambic trimeters, the meter of spoken
verse, but is punctuated by shorter lines at 315 and 318.)*

ANTIGONE:
Zeus! What shall I say? What am I to think, father?   310

OEDIPUS:
What is it, Antigone my child?

ANTIGONE:
                                          I see a woman
approaching close towards us, mounted on
a colt from Aetna;[36] on her head she wears
a Thessalian hat,[37] to keep the sun from her face.
What am I to say?   315
Is it? Or isn't it? Or is my judgement wandering?
Yes... No... I don't know what to say.
I am overcome!
It's no one else! With bright glances from her eyes
she greets me as she approaches, revealing that   320
this is the dear face of none other than Ismene!

OEDIPUS:
What did you say, child?

ANTIGONE:
                                          I see your child, my
sister! You will shortly be able to know her by her voice.

---

36. This refers to a special breed from Sicily, which was famous for its
horses.
37. A kind of broad-brimmed felt traveling hat.

*(Enter Ismene from the direction of Thebes. She probably enters alone
and on foot. We may imagine that she has left her horse with the
attendant mentioned at 334.)*

ISMENE:
Father and sister, sweetest pair
of names to me! After scarcely finding you,   325
now I can scarcely see you for tears of pain!³⁸

OEDIPUS:
Child, have you come?

ISMENE:
                        Father ill-fated to look upon!

OEDIPUS:
Child, have you appeared?

ISMENE:
                        Not without toil for myself.

OEDIPUS:
Come and touch me, child!

ISMENE:
                        I hold you both together.

OEDIPUS:
My own seed, sisters!³⁹

ISMENE:
                        Miserable nurture!⁴⁰   330

OEDIPUS:
You mean hers and mine?

ISMENE:
                        And of my ill-fated self, the third.

OEDIPUS:
Child, why did you come?

ISMENE:
                        Out of concern for you, father.

OEDIPUS:
Was it out of yearning?

ISMENE:
                        And to report in person,
with the only trusty house-slave that I had.

---

38. Ismene's joy is mixed with pain at the wretched condition in which she
    has found her father and sister.
39. The ambiguity of these words reminds us that Oedipus' daughters are
    also his sisters.
40. Ismene is exclaiming at the wretched sustenance of her father and
    sister. "Nurture," especially that of Oedipus, is an important theme in
    the play (see Interpretation p. 94-5).

OEDIPUS:
Where are the young men, your brothers, to share this pain?   335
ISMENE:
They are where they are; dread are their deeds now.
OEDIPUS:
Those two resemble in their nature and life's nurture
in every way the laws that hold in Egypt.[41]
For there the males sit indoors
plying the loom, while their wives   340
ever provide life's nurture from outside.
So with you two, children: those whom these pains befitted
stay home in the house like maidens,
while you two in their place bear painfully the evils
of my unhappy self. For Antigone, since the time   345
she left youth's nurture and gained bodily strength,
ever wandering ill-fated with me
is an old man's guide,[42] often going as a vagrant
through the wild wood, barefoot and unfed,
and often in pouring rain and burning sun,   350
toiling, enduring, she ranks second the comforts
of life at home, if only her father may have nurture.
And you, child,[43] came out before to bring your father
in secret from the Cadmeans,[44] all the prophecies
pronounced concerning my person,[45] and were a trusty   355
guardian of my interests when I was being driven from the land.
    Now this time, Ismene, what tale have you come to bring
your father? What errand has stirred you from home?
For you have not come empty-handed—that I know
clearly—without bringing some dread news for me.   360
ISMENE:
The sufferings that I suffered, father,
while seeking out your place of residence and nurture,
I shall pass over and let go. For I do not wish to grieve twice,

---

41. This passage was probably suggested to Sophocles by the discussion of Egyptian customs at Herodotus 2.35. It ascribes to the Egyptians a total reversal of Greek cultural norms for the division of labor between the sexes, and reflects the Greek tendency to regard foreigners as barbarians whose civilization was morally and intellectually inferior to their own.

42. The word Oedipus uses here (*gerontagogei*) echoes the common Greek word for a schoolboy's attendant (*paidagogos*), thus underlining the reversal of natural roles in the relationship between father and daughter.

43. I.e. Ismene, who has been living at Thebes but has still done all she can to help her exiled father.

44. "Cadmean" means "Theban," after Cadmus, the founder of Thebes.

45. It appears that various prophecies have been made concerning Oedipus during his exile. Ismene brings news of the most recent and significant one (387-94), and Polynices mentions another (1300).

both in feeling the pain and then again in speaking of it.
But the evils that are now surrounding your two   365
ill-fated sons, these have I come to reveal.
At first their passionate desire was to leave
the throne to Creon and not defile the city,
reflecting rationally on the family ruin from long ago,
on how it overwhelmed your miserable house.   370
But now, from some god and a wicked mind,
evil strife has come upon the thrice-miserable pair—
to grasp at rule and autocratic power.[46]
And the younger one, the lesser-born in years,
has bereft the first-born, Polynices,   375
of the throne, and driven him from his fatherland.[47]
But Polynices, according to the general word among us,
after going in exile to the valley of Argos, is mustering
new marriage ties and shield-bearing friends,[48]
planning that Argos will shortly either occupy   380
the Cadmean plain in honor, or raise it to the sky.[49]
These things are no mere string of words, father,
but dreadful deeds. But at what point the gods
will take pity on your pain, I cannot learn.

OEDIPUS:
What, have you now gained hope that the gods will have
some care for me, so that I may one day be saved?

ISMENE:
Yes, father, judging from the recent prophecies.

OEDIPUS:
Which ones are those? What have oracles declared, child?

ISMENE:
That you will one day be sought by the people there,[50]
whether dead or alive, for their own safety.   390

---

46. "Autocrat" and "autocratic" are used in this translation for *tyrannos*
    and related words. Although *tyrannos* gives us the word "tyrant," it does
    not mean a tyrant in our sense, but any absolute ruler, whether benign
    or tyrannical (it is used, for example, of Oedipus in *Oedipus the King*,
    and Creon uses it of himself at 851). This kind of rule was, however, often
    regarded with suspicion, especially by the democratic Athenians, and
    tyrannos can have pejorative overtones. Note that such language is never
    used of Theseus or Athens in this play, but only with reference to Thebes
    (373, 419, 449, 1338).
47. In other versions of the myth Polynices is the younger son (see
    Introduction p. 17).
48. Polynices married the daughter of the king of Argos, thus making the
    Argives his allies. The rest of his allies are listed at 1313-22.
49. I.e. Polynices will either conquer Thebes ("the Cadmean plain") or give
    Thebes the glory of conquering Argos, thus raising Thebes "to the sky."
50. I.e. at Thebes.

OEDIPUS:
But who could prosper through the agency of such a man?

ISMENE:
It is said that their power comes to depend on you.

OEDIPUS:
When I no longer exist, is *that* when I am a man?[51]

ISMENE:
The gods are now raising you up, who before destroyed you.

OEDIPUS:
It's a poor thing to raise in old age one who fell in youth.   395

ISMENE:
Yet know that Creon, at least, for this reason
will come to you shortly—not after untold time.

OEDIPUS:
To do what, daughter? Explain to me.

ISMENE:
To settle you close to the Cadmean land, that they may have
power over you without your entering the land's borders.   400

OEDIPUS:
But what help comes from me lying at the gates?

ISMENE:
Your grave, if it meets misfortune, will weigh heavily on them.[52]

OEDIPUS:
One might learn this much by judgement, without a god's help.

ISMENE:
For this reason, then, they want to settle you near
the country, and not where you may be in your own power.   405

OEDIPUS:
Will they also shade my body with Theban dust?[53]

ISMENE:
But father, the blood of your race does not allow this.[54]

OEDIPUS:
Then never shall they gain power over *me*!

ISMENE:
One day, then, this will weigh heavily on the Cadmeans.

OEDIPUS:
When what circumstance appears, child?   410

51. Oedipus expresses his abject condition by declaring that he no longer
exists (compare 109-10). He takes a dim view of the divine process which
has reduced him to such a state before making him once more "a man"
by giving him power over the lives of others.
52. Ritual offerings were regularly made to placate the dead. The tomb of
a hero, if neglected, was especially dangerous (see Introduction p. 12-13).
53. Oedipus is asking whether he is to be buried in Theban soil.
54. Ismene is referring as delicately as possible to Oedipus' parricide,
which allegedly prevents him from being buried in Theban soil.

ISMENE:
Because of your anger, when they make a stand at your tomb.

OEDIPUS:
From whom did you hear what you are declaring, child?

ISMENE:
From envoys coming from the Delphic hearth.[55]

OEDIPUS:
And did Phoebus really say these things about me?[56]

ISMENE:
So say those returning to the plain of Thebes.   415

OEDIPUS:
Has either of my sons, then, heard these things?

ISMENE:
Both alike, and both understand them well.

OEDIPUS:
Then those most evil ones, hearing these things, placed
autocratic rule above any yearning for me?[57]

ISMENE:
I grieve to hear this, but must bear it nonetheless.   420

OEDIPUS:
Then may the gods not extinguish
their destined strife! And may their end
come to depend on me in this battle
they are now undertaking, raising up their spears!
Then he who now holds the scepter and the throne   425
would not remain, nor would the one who has departed
ever return. For when I who begot them
was being thrust out so dishonorably from my fatherland,
those two did not prevent it or defend me, but let me be
sent forth uprooted, proclaimed by heralds an exile.   430
    You may say the city granted that gift to me
fittingly, since I wanted it at the time.
Not so! For during that first day,
when my rage seethed, and the sweetest thing for me
was death, to be stoned with rocks,   435
no one appeared to help fulfill this passionate desire.
But in time, when all my toil was mitigated,
and I began to learn that my rage had run too far,
chastising my earlier errors to excess,
that was when the city chose to drive me out by force   440

---

55. It was common practice for a city to send envoys to consult oracles,
   especially Apollo's oracle at Delphi, about matters of public importance.
56. On the name Phoebus for Apollo see above, n. 16.
57. Oedipus' sons showed that they valued the throne above their father
   by neglecting him until they discovered that their rule depended on him.
   On "autocracy" see above, n. 46.

from the land, after so much time; and they, though able,
sons of their father, to help their father, were unwilling
to act, and for the lack of a little word from them
I have been roaming abroad, an exiled beggar, ever since.
From these two, who are maidens, I have   445
life's nurture—as far as their nature allows—
and security in the land, and familial aid.
But those two chose above him who begot them a throne,
and sceptered sway, and autocratic rule over the land.
Never, then, shall they win this man as their ally!   450
Nor to them from this Cadmean rule shall benefit
ever come! This I know, both from hearing
this girl's prophecies and reflecting in my mind upon
the age-old sayings Phoebus has fulfilled for me at last.
    Therefore let them send Creon to seek   455
me out, and anyone else with strength in that city.
For if you, strangers, are willing,
with the help of these solemn guardian goddesses,
to give me protection, you will gain for this city
a great savior, and for my enemies, pain.   460

CHORUS LEADER:
  You are worthy of our pity, Oedipus,
  both you and these children here. And since with your words
  you also offer yourself as a savior of this land,
  I wish to counsel you to your advantage.

OEDIPUS:
  Dearest friend, be hospitable, for I will now fulfill all.   465

CHORUS LEADER:
  Perform a purification for these divinities, to whom
  you first came, trampling their soil.

OEDIPUS:
  In what way? Tell me, strangers.

CHORUS LEADER:
  First bring sacred drink-offerings from
  an ever-flowing spring, touching them with holy hands.   470

OEDIPUS:
  And when I have taken this untainted stream?

CHORUS LEADER:
  There are bowls, work of a craftsman's skillful hands—
  wreathe their rims and handles on each side.

OEDIPUS:
  With twigs, or woollen cloths, or in what way?

CHORUS LEADER:
  Taking the freshly-shorn fleece of a young lamb.   475

OEDIPUS:
Very well. But how must I conclude what follows?

CHORUS LEADER:
Pour drink-offerings, standing towards the first dawn.[58]

OEDIPUS:
Should I pour these from the vessels that you spoke of?

CHORUS LEADER:
Yes, in three streams; but empty the last one fully.

OEDIPUS:
With what should I fill this and set it in place? Tell
me this too.   480

CHORUS LEADER:
With water and honey; but do not add wine.[59]

OEDIPUS:
And when the dark-leaved earth has received these offerings?

CHORUS LEADER:
Placing thrice nine sprigs of olive with both hands
upon it, say the following prayer.

OEDIPUS:
This I wish to hear, for it is most important.   485

CHORUS LEADER:
Pray that just as we call them Kindly Ones,[60] with kindly
breasts they may welcome the suppliant savior.
Beg them yourself, or anyone else in your place,
speaking imperceptibly and not crying aloud.
Then move away without turning back.[61] If you do   490
these things, I would stand by you with confidence;
otherwise, stranger, I would feel dread concerning you.[62]

OEDIPUS:
Children, do you two hear these local strangers?

ANTIGONE:
We heard; order us to do what must be done.

---

58. This refers not to the time of day but to the fact that purifying rites were performed facing the east (representing light and purity). Offerings to earth-divinities like the Eumenides were never made until after midday.
59. The Eumenides never received offerings of wine (cf. 100). Honey is a traditional offering to the dead. Wool, water, and the olive were all thought to have purifying power.
60. This is the literal meaning of the name "Eumenides", designed to avert the goddesses' dangerous wrath (see Introduction p. 11).
61. After making offerings to "earth" divinities one had to avert one's eyes (see Introduction p. 11).
62. The chorus are concerned for Oedipus' welfare (cf. 464), but they are also afraid on their own behalf.

OEDIPUS:
The road is closed to me, for I am disabled by   495
my weakness and my lack of sight—twin evils.
But let one of you two go and do these things.
For I think one soul suffices even for untold numbers
in making this payment, if that one is well-disposed.
Quickly, you two, take action! But do not   500
leave me alone. For my body would lack the strength
to move, if left desolate or without a guide.

ISMENE:
I shall go and fulfill the rite. But where shall I find
the necessary spot? This I wish to learn.

CHORUS LEADER:
On the far side of this grove, stranger. But if you   505
lack anything, there is a resident who will tell you.

ISMENE:
I'll go and do it. Antigone, you stay
and guard our father here. For in the cause of parents,
even if one labor painfully, one must not mind the pain.

(Exit Ismene into the grove.)

Strophe A [63]

CHORUS:
It is dreadful, stranger, to awaken   510
the evil now long at rest.
But nonetheless I long passionately to inquire...

OEDIPUS:
What is this?

CHORUS:
...about the wretched distress, found to be
intractable, in which you were involved.

OEDIPUS:
Do not, in the name of your own hospitality,   515
open up the shameless things I suffered!

CHORUS:
But I desire, stranger, to hear a correct account
of this widespread and by no means ceasing tale.

OEDIPUS:
Alas!

CHORUS:
Acquiesce, I supplicate.

OEDIPUS:
Woe! Woe!

---

63. Between the departure of Ismene and the arrival of Theseus (who must
    be played by the same actor) the chorus and Oedipus sing an intensely
    emotional lyric dialogue (510-48).

CHORUS:
Be persuaded, as I was to do all you desired. 520

Antistrophe A

OEDIPUS:
I bore evil, strangers, bore it
against my will—god be my witness!
None of those things was my own choice.

CHORUS:
But in what regard?

OEDIPUS:
The city bound me, who knew nothing, by an evil bed 525
to a marriage that was my doom.

CHORUS:
Was it really with your mother, as I hear,
that you filled your infamous marriage bed?

OEDIPUS:
Alas! It is death to hear those words,
stranger! But these two girls, my own... 530

CHORUS:
What are you saying?

OEDIPUS:
... children, but twin dooms...

CHORUS:
Oh Zeus!

OEDIPUS:
... sprang from a common mother's labor-pains.

Strophe B

CHORUS:
So they are both your offspring and...

OEDIPUS:
Yes, sisters in common with their father. 535

CHORUS:
Oh!

OEDIPUS:
Oh indeed! The wheeling
onslaught of untold evils!

CHORUS:
You suffered...

OEDIPUS:
                    I suffered accursed burdens.

CHORUS:
You did...

OEDIPUS:

    I *did* nothing!

CHORUS:

           What then?

OEDIPUS:

                  I accepted

a gift. If only—my enduring heart!—   540

I had never taken it from the city for my help.[64]

   Antistrophe B

CHORUS:

Unhappy man, what then? Did you commit the murder...

OEDIPUS:

What is this? What do you want to learn?

CHORUS:

...of your father?

OEDIPUS:

        Ah! A second

stroke! Anguish upon anguish![65]

CHORUS:

You killed...

OEDIPUS:

      I killed. But I have...   545

CHORUS:

What is this?

OEDIPUS:

      ... a just defence.

CHORUS:

           What then?

OEDIPUS:

                I shall tell you:

in folly I murdered and destroyed him,

but pure under the law, I reached this point unknowingly.

(Enter Theseus from the direction of Athens. The lyric dialogue ends, and the meter returns to iambic trimeters.)

CHORUS LEADER:

But here is our lord, the offspring of Aegeus,

Theseus, who was sent for at your word.   550

THESEUS:

Having heard from many in time gone by

---

64. Oedipus received the throne of Thebes and the hand of Jocasta as a reward for saving the city from the Sphinx (see Introduction p. 15).

65. The word translated "anguish" here and below (598, 765) literally means "sickness" or "disease"—a common Greek metaphor for mental suffering.

of the bloody destruction of your eyes,
I recognized you, child of Laius; and now too, hearing
more along this road, I further understand.
For both your attire and your unhappy face   555
make plain to us that you are who you are. And pitying you
I want to ask, ill-fated Oedipus, with what
entreaty for the city or myself you have stopped here,
you and your ill-fated attendant.
Tell me. For dread would be the deed you could succeed   560
in mentioning, from which *I* would stand aside—
I who know that I too was reared as a stranger,
like you, and that I struggled in a strange land
against uniquely numerous perils to my life,[66]
so that from no one who is a stranger, like you now,   565
would I turn away without helping to save him. For
I know well that I am a man, and that of tomorrow's
day I have no greater share than you.

OEDIPUS:
Theseus, your nobility has in few words
spared me any shame at speaking briefly.   570
For who I am, and from what father born,
and from what land arrived, you have accurately said,
so that nothing more remains for me except
to say what I desire, and then my words are done.

THESEUS:
Then tell me this very thing, that I may learn.   575

OEDIPUS:
I come to give my miserable body to you
as a gift. It is not excellent to look upon, but
the profits from it are better than fine appearance.

THESEUS:
What kind of profit do you claim to have brought?

OEDIPUS:
You may learn in time, but not, I think, at present.   580

THESEUS:
At what time, then, will your offering be made plain?

---

66. Theseus was "reared as a stranger" because he was raised by his
mother, Aethra, at her home in Troezen in the Peloponnese (see map of
mainland Greece below, p. 82), without knowing that his father was king
of Athens. On reaching adulthood he traveled to his father's home,
performing many heroic deeds along the way (the "perils to my life").
Similarly Oedipus was raised in Corinth by his adopted father Polybus,
not knowing that his natural father Laius was king of Thebes. On
discovering his true identity he suffered great misery, including his
present wanderings as a stranger. Theseus manages to emphasize tact-
fully the experiences that unite them without touching on the qualitative
difference in their misfortunes.

OEDIPUS:
When I die and you lay me in my tomb.

THESEUS:
So you beg life's last rites, and what comes between
you either forget or value at nothing.

OEDIPUS:
Yes, for in this the rest is harvested for me.[67]   585

THESEUS:
This favor that you beg of me is slight.

OEDIPUS:
But look out! This is no small struggle, no!

THESEUS:
Do you mean between me and your offspring?

OEDIPUS:
They will have me conveyed by necessity to Thebes.

THESEUS:
But if you want to go, then exile for you is no fine thing.   590

OEDIPUS:
But when I wanted this myself, they did not allow it.

THESEUS:
Foolish man, rage is no advantage among evils.

OEDIPUS:
When you have learned from me, advise, but for now let me be.

THESEUS:
Inform me. For I must not speak without judgement.

OEDIPUS:
I have suffered, Theseus, dreadful evils upon evils.   595

THESEUS:
Do you mean the age-old fate of your family?

OEDIPUS:
No indeed. For every Greek cries that aloud.

THESEUS:
What then is your anguish beyond the human scale?

OEDIPUS:
This is my condition: I was driven from my land
by my own seed; I am never   600
again to return, because of my parricide.

THESEUS:
Then how could they send you there, if you must reside apart?

OEDIPUS:
The lips of the god lay necessity upon them.

---

67. Oedipus means that if he is promised burial in Attica the remainder
   of his life is also secure, since Theseus must protect him from any threat
   of abduction.

THESEUS:
What suffering do they dread from oracles?

OEDIPUS:
That they must by necessity be struck down in this land   605

THESEUS:
And how could my dealings with them turn bitter?

OEDIPUS:
Dearest child of Aegeus, to the gods alone
old age comes not, nor death,
but all-powerful time confounds all other things.
Earth's strength decays, the body's strength decays,   610
trust dies, distrustfulness springs up,
and the same spirit never stays constant
between men who are friends or from city to city.
For to some now, to others at a later time
delightful things turn bitter and then dear again.   615
So too with Thebes: if all between you now
is fine and tranquil weather, yet untold time
gives birth in its course to untold nights and days,
in which they will scatter with the spear their present
harmonious pledges, for some little cause.   620
And there my sleeping and concealed cold
corpse will one day drink up their hot blood,
if Zeus is still Zeus and Phoebus, son of Zeus, speaks clear.
But—for it does not please me to tell the inviolable words[68]—
allow me to end where I began. Only guard   625
your trust, and never will you say you welcomed
Oedipus as a useless resident of this
region—if the gods do not play me false.

CHORUS:
Lord, this man has long appeared as one who will fulfill
both these words and others like them for this land.   630

THESEUS:
Who then would cast out the kindness[69] of such
a man? First, a common hearth of spear-
friendship with us is always open to him.[70]
Moreover, arriving as a suppliant of the gods,
he pays to this land and me no little tribute.   635
Revering these things, never shall I cast out the favor
of this man, but shall make him a resident of our city and country.

---

68. The precise details of Oedipus' fate are "inviolable" because they must
remain secret.
69. This word (*eumeneia*) is often used for the good will of the gods, and
echoes the name of the Eumenides (see Introduction p. 11 and cf. 486-7).
70. Theseus is referring to a pre-existing military alliance between the
royal houses of Athens and Thebes.

If it pleases the stranger to stay here, I shall
command you to guard him,[71] or he may proceed with me.
Whichever of these pleases you, Oedipus, I give you   640
the choice to do it. For I shall agree with your decision.

OEDIPUS:
Zeus, may you reward such people well!

THESEUS:
What then do you desire? To proceed to my house?

OEDIPUS::
If it were permitted for me. But this is the place...

THESEUS:
Where you will do what? I shall not stand in your way.   645

OEDIPUS:
... where I shall overpower those who cast me out.

THESEUS:
The gift you speak of from your presence would be great.

OEDIPUS:
Yes, if what *you* say remains fulfilled for me by you.

THESEUS:
In me at least have confidence. Never shall I betray you.

OEDIPUS:
I shall not bind your trust under oath, as I would an evil man.   650

THESEUS:
You would gain nothing further than by my word.

OEDIPUS:
What then will you do?

THESEUS:
                        From what exactly do you cower?

OEDIPUS:
Men will come...

THESEUS:
                    These people will take care of that.

OEDIPUS:
Look out, lest leaving me...

THESEUS:
                        Don't tell me what I must do.

OEDIPUS:
It is necessary for one who cowers...

THESEUS:
                            My heart cowers not.   655

OEDIPUS:
You do not know the threats...

---

71. Theseus is addressing the chorus.

THESEUS:
                    I do know that no man
will take you from here by force against my will.
Many threats speak many threatening words
in vain from rage. But when the mind
gains control of itself, those threatenings are gone.   660
So too perhaps with them: even if boldness prompted dreadful words
of taking you away, the sea-voyage here, I know,
will turn out long and hard to sail.[72]
Now I counsel you to have confidence,
even apart from my resolve, if Phoebus sent you.   665
But nonetheless, even in my absence, I know that
my name will guard you from suffering any evil.

(Exit Theseus, in the direction of Colonus and Athens.)

Strophe A [73]

CHORUS:
In this country of fine horses, stranger,
you have reached the mightiest shelter upon earth,
white Colonus.[74]   670
The clear-toned nightingale,
frequenting it most,
pipes plaintively within green glades,
occupying the wine-dark ivy
and the foliage of the god   675
where none may step, with untold berries, out of the sun,
out of the wind of all
storms.[75] Within it Dionysus
the Bacchic reveller ever steps,
in company with his divine nurses.[76]   680

Antistrophe A
Under the heavenly dew
ever flourishes, day by day, the fine-clustered

---

72. This is a metaphor, since the journey from Thebes to Athens is over land (see map of Attica below, p. 89). The sea and sailing are common sources of metaphor among the Greeks (a sea-faring people), especially for risky undertakings (cf. 1746).

73. The chorus now dance and sing their first stasimon ("song in position") (668-719). The first strophic pair (i.e. strophe plus antistrophe) is devoted to Colonus, and the second to Attica more generally. The song marks and celebrates the moment of Oedipus' formal acceptance by Theseus as an Athenian citizen (637).

74. The soil at Colonus was light in color.

75. The "god" in this sentence is Dionysus, to whom ivy, grape-vines and other plants were sacred. Besides his role as patron of the theater, he was a god of fertility and vegetation, especially the vine.

76. The infant Dionysus was nursed by nymphs, who subsequently remained his companions in the Bacchic revelry that was distinctive of him and his cult.

narcissus—the ancient crown
of the two great goddesses—and the
gold-beaming crocus.[77] Nor do the   685
sleepless springs diminish,
distributing the stream
of Cephisus,[78] but each day,
bringing swift fertility, it ever reaches the plains
of the broad-breasted earth   690
with untainted flood. Nor do
the Muses' choruses abhor this land, nor again
does Aphrodite of the golden reins.[79]

Strophe B

And there is something such as I
do not hear of in the land of Asia,[80]   695
or springing up in the great
Dorian isle of Pelops,[81]
a self-generating growth, unconquered by any hand,
source of fear to hostile spears,[82]
which flourishes most greatly in this country: 700
the foliage of the grey, child-nurturing olive.
This no one, youthful or dwelling
with old age, will nullify with ravaging hand. For
the ever-seeing eye
of Zeus Morios looks upon it,[83]   705
and grey-eyed Athena.

---

77. The narcissus was sacred to Demeter and Persephone, the two great
goddesses of the underworld, and was associated with death. The crocus
and the nightingale (mentioned in the strophe) also symbolize death, as
befits the place where Oedipus will die.
78. Cephisus is a river flowing through Attica to the west of Athens, not
far from Colonus (see map of Attica below, p. 89).
79. Aphrodite, goddess of erotic desire, was sometimes portrayed as
driving a golden chariot drawn by birds (sparrows, doves or swans).
80. To the Greeks "Asia" signified what is now the Middle East.
81. "Isle of Pelops" is the literal meaning of "Peloponnese," the southern
Greek peninsula largely inhabited by Dorian Greeks. Olives did of course
grow here and in "Asia", but the first tree did not "spring up" there (see
next note).
82. Attic legend had it that the first olive tree sprang from the Acropolis
in Athens at the command of Athena. Certain olive trees were sacred,
including one on the Acropolis, which was said to have returned miracu-
lously to life after burning during the Persian wars (hence "self-generating"). It was also said that later invaders had spared the sacred olives
because they were under the protection of Athena (hence "source of fear").
"Conquered by no hand" could allude to either or both of these stories.
83. "Morios" is the title of Zeus as protector of the sacred olives.

Antistrophe B
Another mightiest tale of praise
have I to tell for this mother-city:
the gifts of the great divinity,[84]
greatest boast of the land,   710
fine horses, fine colts, fine sea.
For you, child of Cronos,[85] enthroned
our city on this boast; you, Lord Poseidon,
who instituted the bridle, cure of wild horses,
in these streets first.   715
And the fine sea-faring oar-blade,
fitted to the hand,
leaps marvelously, following
the hundred feet of the Nereids.[86]

(The chorus end their song and dance. Enter Creon, with an armed escort, from the direction of Thebes.)

ANTIGONE:
Oh soil most eulogized with praises,   720
now it is yours to manifest those shining words in deeds!

OEDIPUS:
What fresh thing is upon us, child?

ANTIGONE:
                              Here is Creon coming
close to us, and not without an escort, father.

OEDIPUS:
Dearest old men, it is from you
that my ultimate safety may now appear.   725

CHORUS LEADER:
Have confidence, it shall be here! For even if I am old,
this country's strength has not reached old age.

CREON:
Gentlemen, noble residents of this land,
I see that you have got some sudden fear
within your eyes at my approach.   730
But do not cower from me, or let fly evil words.
For I have not come wishing to take action, since
I am old, and understand that I have come
to a city whose strength, if any in Hellas, is great.[87]
But I have been dispatched, at my age, to persuade   735

84. This "great divinity" is Poseidon, god of the sea and of horses.
85. Poseidon was son of Cronos and Rhea, who, according to Hesiod, were also the parents of Zeus, Hades and Hera.
86. The fifty sea-nymphs known as Nereids are the daughters of the sea-god Nereus. They are sometimes portrayed as escorting ships through the waves.
87. "Hellas" is the Greek name for Greece.

this man to follow me back to Cadmean soil—
not dispatched by one man, but commanded
by all the citizens, since it devolved on me by family ties
to mourn this man's troubles most of all the city.
    Long-suffering Oedipus, hear me   740
and come home! The whole Cadmean people
calls you with justice, and of them most myself,
just as I, unless I am of all humans by nature
the most evil, grieve most at your evils, old man,
seeing you, unhappy one, being a stranger   745
and going always as a vagrant, bereft of livelihood,
relying on one attendant, who I—woe is me!—
never thought would fall into such a state of
outrage, as that into which this ill-fated girl has fallen,
always tending you and your blind face,   750
with a beggar's way of life, at her age, with no experience
of marriage, but there for any passing man to seize.[88]
    Is this reproach not miserable—woe is me!—
that I have cast at you and me and all our family?
But—for it is impossible to conceal what is manifest—   755
by your paternal gods, Oedipus, be persuaded and
conceal it now, by going willingly to your paternal
city and home, having said a friend's farewell to this
city; for it deserves it; but more reverence is justly
due to your home city, which is your nurse from long ago.   760

OEDIPUS:
You would dare anything! You would make
a crafty scheme out of any just argument!
Why do you attempt this, and want to capture me
a second time, where capture would most greatly grieve me?
For before, when I was in anguish with my home-grown   765
evils, and my delight was to be thrown out of the land,
you did not want to bestow this favor on one wanting it;[89]
but when I had already had my fill of rage,
and it was sweet to me to pass my life within the house,
then you decided to thrust me forth and cast me out, nor   770
was this "family tie" in any way dear to you *then*.
And now again, when you see that this city

---

88. The extreme length and complexity of this sentence contribute to the
artifice of Creon's rhetoric. Note that the final words ironically fore-
shadow his own behavior (see 818-9).

89. These events are dramatized at the end of *Oedipus the King*, where
Creon refuses to let Oedipus go into exile without first consulting the
Delphic oracle. Oedipus' account here suggests that no such consultation
occurred, making his subsequent exile appear arbitrary and cruel. But
exile was the traditional penalty for bloodshed (compare 407), and in the
earlier play Oedipus himself curses the killer of Laius with exile (*Oedipus
the King* 236-51).

at my side is well-disposed to me, and this whole race,[90]
you attempt to drag me back, using soft words to say harsh things.
Yet what delight is there in being loved against one's will?   775
As if when you begged persistently to get something
someone should give you nothing, and not want to aid you,
but when your heart was full of your desire, *then*
he should make the gift, when the favor could win no favor.
Would you not find such a pleasure vain?   780
Yet such is what you are offering to me—
things good in word, but evil in the doing.
    I shall tell these people too, to make your evil plain:
you have come to take me, not so as to take me home,
but so that you may make me resident nearby, and your city   785
may escape, undoomed by evils from this land.
Yet that is not your lot, but this is yours: my avenging
spirit over that country, dwelling there always.
And this is for my children:[91] to get
just this much of my land—to die in it.   790
Do I not understand things at Thebes better than you?
Much better, just as I also hear from clearer sources,
Phoebus and Zeus himself, who is his father.
Your counterfeit lips have come here
with a very sharp edge.[92] But your words   795
may win you more evil than safety.
But—for I know I am not persuading you—go!
And leave us to live here. For our life, even as we are,
would not be evil, if we could take delight in it.

CREON:
Do you think your response is a misfortune for me,
or rather for yourself, in our present argument?   801

OEDIPUS:
The sweetest thing for me is for you to fail
to persuade either me or these nearby people.

CREON:
Ill-fated man, will you never, even with time, manifest
some native sense? Are you nurtured as a blight upon old age?   805

OEDIPUS:
You are dreadfully clever with your tongue; but I know

90. "Race" translates *genos*, which also means "family" (738, 753). The Athenians have replaced the race and family that disowned Oedipus, making Creon's overtures futile.
91. In Greek the masculine gender of the word "children" makes it clear that Oedipus is speaking of his sons, not his daughters. But the masculine can also be used for sons and daughters collectively. We may recall that Antigone too will die in the land of Thebes, as an indirect result of her father's curse. There is the same irony in the word "children" at 1396.
92. In the Greek there is a pun on the word *stoma*, which can mean "mouth" or "edge."

no just man who speaks well on every subject.

CREON:
To speak much and to speak opportunely are different.

OEDIPUS:
As if you spoke briefly, and that opportunely!

CREON:
Not indeed to one with as little mind as you!   810

OEDIPUS:
Be gone!—I shall speak for these people too—and do not
guard me with a blockade where I must dwell.

CREON:
I call these people, not you, to witness what words you give
in answer to your friends. If ever I capture you...

OEDIPUS:
Who, despite these allies, would capture me by force?   815

CREON:
Indeed, even without that you will be in pain.

OEDIPUS:
With what deed behind it have you made this threat?

CREON:
Of your two children I have just seized
and sent away one, and shall soon take the other.[93]

OEDIPUS:
Alas!

CREON:
       You will soon have more reason for this "alas."   820

OEDIPUS:
You have my child?

CREON:
               And this one too before long!

OEDIPUS:
Oh strangers! What will you do? Will you betray me,
and not drive this irreverent man from the land?

CHORUS:
Get out, stranger, quickly! For what you are now
doing is not just, nor was what you did before.   825

(Creon addresses his men.)

CREON:
Now is your opportunity to take this girl away—
against her will, if she will not travel willingly.

---

93. We may imagine that Creon secretly kidnapped Ismene from the grove
before his entrance. Alternatively he may have silently sent a guard to
do so earlier in this scene, but this is nowhere signalled in the text and
might spoil the surprise of Creon's announcement here.

(Creon and his men approach Antigone.)

ANTIGONE:
Alas! Woe is me! Where can I flee? What protection
can I get from gods or mortals?

CHORUS:
What are you doing, stranger?

CREON:
I shall not touch this man, but only her who is my own.[94]   830

(He seizes Antigone.)

OEDIPUS:
Lords of the land!

CHORUS:
Stranger, your deed is unjust!

CREON:
It is just.

CHORUS:
How just?

CREON:
I am taking my own.

Strophe [95]

OEDIPUS:
Oh city!

CHORUS:
What are you doing, stranger? Won't you let her go? Soon
you will come to the test of blows.   835

CREON:
Keep away!

CHORUS:
Not from you, while this is your design.

CREON:
You will battle with my city, if you cause me any trouble.

OEDIPUS:
Did I not say this would happen?

---

94. In *Oedipus the King,* Oedipus leaves his daughters in Thebes under
Creon's protection (1503-10). But in *Oedipus at Colonus* his claim to his
nieces' guardianship can scarcely apply to Antigone, who has been
wandering with her father for many years.

95. At this climactic moment the scene is punctuated by a lyric dialogue,
in which the strophe (833-43) is separated from the antistrophe (876-86)
by some thirty lines of spoken dialogue (844-75). The division of many of
the lines between more than one speaker gives an impression of excited
confusion, which is enhanced in the lyrics by the use of dochmiacs, a
metre often used to express emotional agitation.

CHORUS:

Release the child
from your hands, quickly!

CREON:

Do not command where you lack power.

CHORUS:
I tell you to free her!

(Creon hands Antigone over to his men, to whom his next words are addressed.)

CREON:

And I tell you to start your journey.   840

(Creon's men start to drag Antigone towards the road to Thebes.)

CHORUS:
Come here! Come, come, people of this place!
The city is being destroyed, my city, by strength![96]
Come here, I beg!

ANTIGONE:
I am dragged unhappily away! Oh strangers, strangers![97]

OEDIPUS:
Where are you, my child?

ANTIGONE:

I am forced to travel away!   845

OEDIPUS:
Hold out your hands, child!

ANTIGONE:

I have no strength!

(Creon addresses his men.)

CREON:
Won't you take her away?

OEDIPUS:

Woe! Woe is me!

(Exeunt Creon's men, with Antigone, in the direction of Thebes.)

CREON:
Never again will you journey leaning on *those*

---

96. Athens is not literally under attack, but its authority is being undermined by the violation of sanctuary and abduction of a suppliant (compare 879).

97. These words are addressed to the chorus. The Greek word *xenos*, translated throughout as "stranger," can also mean "host," "guest," or "guest-friend." Those who welcome a stranger initiate guest-friendship, a relationship based on mutual hospitality. The word "stranger" may thus have friendly overtones, depending on the context.

two scepters![98] But since you want to conquer
your fatherland and friends, at whose command   850
I do these deeds—autocrat though I am[99]—
then conquer! For in time, I know, you will recognize this:
that what you are now doing to yourself is not
fine, nor was what you did before, forcibly despite your friends
giving favor to your anger, which always blights you.[100]   855

(Creon starts to follow his men, but the chorus confront him.)

CHORUS LEADER:
Stop there, stranger!

CREON:
                    I tell you not to touch me!

CHORUS LEADER:
I shall not let you go, while I am bereft of those girls.

CREON:
Then you will pay an even greater pledge to my city
soon. For I shall not lay hands on those two alone.

CHORUS LEADER:
To what will you turn?

CREON:
                    I shall catch this man and take him away.   860

CHORUS LEADER:
Dread words!

CREON:
                    Which will now become deeds!

CHORUS LEADER:
Unless the ruler of this land prevents you.

OEDIPUS:
Oh shameless voice, will you really touch *me*?

CREON:
I tell you to be silent!

---

98. Since a scepter is in origin a staff or walking-stick, the same word is
    used in Greek for both. Sophocles exploits this ambiguity to create a
    pathetic contrast between Oedipus' helplessness (here and at 1109) and
    his sons' bid for the royal scepter of Thebes (425, 449, 1354). There is also
    a nice dramatic irony in Creon's words, since as it turns out, Oedipus will
    not need the support of these "scepters" any longer.
99. It is not clear who is presently ruling at Thebes. Creon held power
    after Oedipus blinded himself, but Eteocles recently took the throne from
    Polynices (375-6). We should not press the point. What matters for this
    scene is that Creon represents the powers that be at Thebes, whether or
    not he is currently its "autocrat" (on this word see above, n. 46).
100. In *Oedipus the King*, Oedipus is portrayed as a quick-tempered man
    who turns angrily on various friends, including Creon. The most clearly
    self-destructive consequences of this passionate spirit are the killing of
    Laius (*Oedipus the King* 806-813) and Oedipus' self-blinding (1268-70;
    cf. *Oedipus at Colonus* 433-9, 1195-1200).

OEDIPUS:
No! May these divinities
not stop me from speaking this further curse,[101]   865
on you, most evil one, who have wrenched away by force
my unarmed eye, before my sightless eyes, and gone with her.[102]
Therefore may Helios, the god who looks on all,[103] grant
that you yourself and your family too
live out some day an old age such as mine.[104]   870

CREON:
Do you see this, local people of this land?

OEDIPUS:
They see both me and you, and understand that
having suffered deeds I am requiting you with words.

CREON:
I shall no longer restrain my rage, but shall take by force
this man, even though I am alone and slowed by time.   875

Antistrophe

OEDIPUS:
Oh woe is me!

CHORUS:
What audacity you have come with, stranger, if
you think you will fulfill this!

CREON:
I do think so!

CHORUS:
Then I shall no longer consider this a city.

CREON:
In just causes even the slight conquers the great.   880

---

101. Oedipus has already cursed his sons (421-7). For this further curse
on Creon he seeks the approval of the goddesses of the grove, who
sometimes appear as guarantors of curses (see Introduction p 11). Note
that in such contexts Oedipus avoids calling them by the benevolent local
name of Eumenides (cf. 1010, 1391).

102. "Gone with" here and below (895, 1009) is a rhetorical exaggeration,
expressing the finality of the abduction from Oedipus' perspective.

103. Helios is the god of the sun, sometimes identified with Apollo (see
above, n. 16). He is portrayed as traveling through the sky in a golden
chariot, and hence seeing everything that happens on the earth.

104. In ordinary life as well as myth, curses were believed to be powerful
weapons and were much used against personal enemies. It is common to
curse one's enemies with the same evils that they have inflicted on
oneself, as Oedipus does here. Sophocles' earlier play *Antigone* dramatizes some of the disasters that befell Creon in his later years, including
the suicides of his wife and son. Curses are not always effective, in life
or literature, but Oedipus' curses have a special power, since he is an
emerging cult-hero.

OEDIPUS:
Do you hear the words he utters?

CHORUS:
But he will not fulfill them.

* * * * *105

CREON:
Zeus may know that, but not you.

CHORUS:
Is this not an outrage?

CREON:
An outrage you must put up with.

CHORUS:
Oh! All people! *Oh!* Chief men of the land!
Come quickly, come! For those men   885
are already crossing the frontier.

(Enter Theseus, with attendants, from the direction of Colonus.)

THESEUS:
Whatever is this outcry? What deed is afoot? Fearing what
did you stop me at the altar as I sacrificed to the sea-god,
protector of Colonus here? Speak, that I may know the whole affair,
for which I rushed here faster than pleased my feet.   890

OEDIPUS:
Dearest friend—for I recognize your voice—
I have just suffered dreadful things at this man's hand.

THESEUS:
What things? Who is it that has troubled you? Speak!

OEDIPUS:
Creon here, whom you see, has wrenched away
from me my only pair of children and gone with them.106   895

THESEUS:
What did you say?

OEDIPUS:
You have heard exactly what I suffered.

(Theseus addresses his retinue.)

THESEUS:
Won't one of you attendants go as quickly as possible
to that altar, and lay necessity on all the people,
both horseless and on horseback, to hurry from
the sacrifice with slackened rein, to the point where   900
the mouths of the two travelers' roads flow together,107

---

105. Two or three words are missing from the text here.
106. Oedipus no longer counts his sons as his children (cf. 1323-4, 1369, 1383).
107. It is impossible to determine the exact location of this crossroads, somewhere between Athens and Thebes, where the subsequent battle is supposed to take place.

that the girls may not pass, and I may not become
a source of laughter to this stranger, having been subdued by force.
Go, as I bid you, quickly!

(He turns towards Creon.)
                As for this man,
if I had reached the pitch of anger he deserves,   905
I would not let him go unwounded from my hand;
as it is, he shall be disciplined with those laws
that he himself brought with him, and no others.

(He addresses Creon.)
For you shall never leave this country, until
you take those girls and set them clearly here before me.   910
For you have perpetrated deeds unworthy of me,
of those who begot you, and of your own land—
coming into a city that practices justice
and rules on nothing without law, and then, dismissing
this land's authorities and falling on it thus,   915
taking what you desire and possessing it by force.
You thought my city empty of men
or some slave-city, and myself a nothing.
    And yet it was not Thebes that reared you to be evil.
For it does not love to nurture unjust men,   920
nor would it praise you, if it should discover
that you are robbing what is mine and the gods', taking
by force a suppliant band of miserable people.
I for one would not step into your land,
not even if I had the most just cause of all,   925
and without permission from the land's ruler, whoever he was,
plunder or take anything; I would understand
how a stranger should behave among citizens.
But you are shaming your own city,
which does not deserve it, and increasing time   930
is making you together old and mindless.
    Well then. I said it before, and I declare it now:
let someone bring the children here as quickly as possible,
unless you want to be a resident of this country
by force against your will. I say this to you   935
from my mind as well as with my tongue.

CHORUS:
Do you see what you have come to, stranger? From your origins
you *appear* just, but your *deeds* are found to be evil.

CREON:
It was not because I thought this city without men,
son of Aegeus, or without counsel, as you say,   940
that I did this deed, but recognizing that
no eagerness for my blood-kin would ever drive
its people to nurture him by force against my will.

And I knew they would not welcome a man who was
both a parricide and impure, nor one in company with whom   945
was found the impious marriage of a mother with her child.
For I knew they had the well-counseling hill
of Ares in their land, which does not allow
such vagrants to dwell together with this city.[108]
Putting my trust in that, I undertook this hunt.   950
And I would not have done so, if he had not cursed
bitter curses on myself and on my family.
In return for that, having suffered, I thought fit to act.
For rage has no old age other than
death; but the dead are touched by no distress.   955
        You, therefore, will do whatever you want. For
isolation, though I speak justly,
makes me weak. But nonetheless against your deeds,
even at my age, I shall attempt to act in return.

OEDIPUS:
Oh shameless audacity! On which old man do you think   960
you are committing this outrage, myself or you?—
you who have let fly from your lips at me the murder
and the marriage and the fate that—woe is me!—
I bore against my will![109] For so it was dear to the gods,
perhaps in wrath at my family for something long ago.[110]   965
For in myself you could not find any fault
to reproach me with, in return for which
I came to commit these faults against myself and mine.
Tell me, if some divine ordinance from oracles
was approaching my father, that he die at his children's hands,   970
how could you justly reproach *me* with that,
who had not yet sprung into birth from father
or mother, but was at that time unbegotten?
And if again when I appeared, as I unhappily did,
I came to blows with my father and killed him,   975
knowing nothing of what I was doing or to whom I was doing it,
how could you fittingly find fault with this unwilling deed?
And have you no shame, brazen one, at making it necessary
for me to speak of my mother's—your own sister's!—marriage,

---

108. Creon is referring to the Council of the Areopagus (literally, "hill of
Ares"), a very ancient Athenian court with jurisdiction over murder and
religious pollution, which met on a rocky hill near the acropolis. He is
wrong, however, in thinking that the Areopagus would oblige Athens to
reject a suppliant like Oedipus (see further Interpretation p. 98).
109. For the meaning of "against my will" and "unwilling," here and below
(977, 987), see n. 33.
110. On Oedipus' family curse see Introduction p. 15.

when it was such as I shall soon describe? For I shall not stay
   silent,   980
when you have gone this far with your unholy lips!
She bore me, yes, she bore me—alas, alas for my evils!
Unknowing she bore unknowing me, and having done so,
to her own reproach she gave birth to my children.
But one thing I know well, that you are willfully   985
maligning thus myself and her, while I both
unwillingly married her, and utter this unwillingly.
I shall not indeed be called evil, either for this
marriage or for my father's murder, which you always
bring against me, reproaching me bitterly.   990
For answer me just one thing that I ask you:
if someone should come up to you—you, the just man!—
and try here and now to kill you, would you inquire whether
the killer was your father, or repay him at once?
I think, if you love to live, you would repay   995
the man responsible, and not scrutinize the justice of the case.
Yet such were the evils into which I stepped,
with the gods leading me;[111] so that I think not even
my father's soul, were it alive, would contradict me.
But you—for you are not just, but think anything   1000
is fine to say, the speakable and unspeakable alike—
you reproach me thus in front of these people!
 And you think it a fine thing to flatter the name of Theseus,
and Athens, saying how finely it is governed.
Yet among so many praises you forget one thing,   1005
that if any land understands how to revere
the gods with honors, this land excels in doing so,
from which, kidnapping me, an old man and a suppliant,
you tried to take myself and have taken and gone with the girls.
In return for that now, calling upon these goddesses,   1010
I supplicate and assail them with prayers
to come to me as defenders and allies, that you may learn
by what kind of men this city is protected!

CHORUS:
 The stranger, lord, is a good man. His fate
 has been ruinous, but is worthy of defense.   1015

THESEUS:
 Enough words! Those who did the deed
 are hurrying, while we who suffered it are standing still.

CREON:
 What then do you command a feeble man to do?

THESEUS:
 Lead the way down the road they took, going as my
 escort, so that if you have the children in this   1020

111. See note 34.

region, you yourself may come and show them to me.
But if your men are fleeing with them in their power, there is no
        need for our pains;
for there are others to hurry, from whom your men will never
flee out of this country to pray to the gods in gratitude.
Guide the way! Know that you, the captor, are captured,[112]   1025
and fortune has caught you, the hunter. For things
acquired by unjust deception are not kept safe.
Nor will you have anyone else to help you; for I know well
that you did not come unarmed or unequipped to such a point
of outrage in your present deed of daring,   1030
but that you trusted in someone when doing this.
These things I must search out, and not make
this city weaker than a single man.
Do you understand any of this, or do words now seem
as vainly said to you as when you planned this scheme?   1035

CREON:
Nothing you say here will win complaint from me;
but at home we too shall know what we must do.

THESEUS:
Go onward now with your threats! But you, Oedipus,
please stay here at your ease, with my trusty pledge
that unless I die first, I shall not stop   1040
until I place your children under your authority.

OEDIPUS:
May you benefit, Theseus, thanks to your nobility
and your just concern for us!

(Exeunt Theseus, his attendants, and Creon, in the direction of Thebes.)

Strophe A [113]

CHORUS:
If only I were where the hostile
men, wheeling at bay, will soon   1045
mingle in bronze-shouting
Ares,[114] on the Pythian

---

112. "The captors are captured" was a proverbial expression for such
reversals.
113. The chorus dance and sing the second *stasimon* (1044-1095), which
again consists of two strophic pairs. It imaginatively recreates the
confrontation between Creon's and Theseus' men, which takes place
simultaneously. It thus represents a considerable stretch of dramatic
time (see Interpretation p. 99). The geographical references, which
contribute to the play's detailed evocation of Athens and its environs,
would be easily recognized by the original audience.
114. The name of Ares, god of war, is often used for warfare (as here) or a
warlike spirit (as at 1065).

or the torch-lit shores,[115]
where the Ladies nurse
the solemn rites   1050
for mortals on whose tongue
a golden lock has been imposed
by the attendant Eumolpidae.[116]
There, I think, Theseus
the battle-rouser and the traveling pair   1055
of maiden sisters
will soon mingle, with opposing shout,
within this region.

Antistrophe A

Or perhaps they will approach
the land west of the snowy rock,[117]   1060
from the pastures of Oea,
on colts, or fleeing
with the rivalry of swift chariots.
He will be caught! Dread
is the Ares of these local people,   1065
dread the prime of Theseus' men.
For every bridle flashes,
and every mounted
combatant rushes
with slackened rein, all who honor   1070
Athena, goddess of horses,[118]
and the earth-embracing sea-god,
Rhea's dear son.[119]

Strophe B

Are they in action, or about to be? How
my judgement woos me to think   1075

115. The "Pythian shores" are near Daphne, about six miles from Colonus
(see map of Attica below, p. 89), where there was a temple of Apollo, one
of whose titles was "Pythian." The "torch-lit shores" are about five miles
further on, at Eleusis, the site of an annual torch-lit procession in honor
of the two goddesses of the underworld, Demeter and Persephone, who
were often called simply "the Ladies." Their rites, known as the Mysteries, held out the prospect of blissful immortality, and were a secret to all
but their initiates.
116. The priest who carried out the initiation and imposed the pledge of
silence was always a member of the family of the Eumolpidae, in which
the office was hereditary.
117. The text is difficult here, but the "snowy rock" is probably Mount
Aigaleos, to the west of which lay the Athenian rural district or deme of
Oea (see map of Attica below, p. 83).
118. As goddess of horses, Athena shared an altar at Colonus to Poseidon
in his capacity as god of horses. This is presumably the altar where
Theseus has been sacrificing.
119. On the parentage of Poseidon see above, n. 85.

that soon I shall be face to face
with the two who have endured dread things, and found
dread sufferings from their own blood-kin!
Zeus will fulfill, fulfill something this day!
I prophesy a successful struggle.   1080
If only, as a quick strong whirlwind dove,
I might reach this struggle
from an airy cloud,
lifting up my eyes!

Antistrophe B
Oh all-ruling lord of the gods, all-   1085
seeing Zeus! May you grant that
the guardians of this land
fulfill with conquering strength
good hunting in their ambush,
you and your solemn child, Pallas Athena.   1090
And I wish Apollo
the hunter, and his sister who follows
the densely-dappled swift-footed
deer,[120] to come as a double
defense to this land and its citizens.   1095

*(Enter Theseus and his attendants, with Antigone and Ismene, from
the direction of Thebes.)*

CHORUS LEADER:
Vagrant stranger, you will not tell the watchman
that he is a false prophet. For I see the girls
here close by, escorted back this way by attendants.

OEDIPUS:
Where? Where? What are you saying? What did you say?

ANTIGONE:
                        Father, father!
Which of the gods might grant you to see this best   1100
of men, who has sent us back here to you?

OEDIPUS:
Child, are you two really here?

ANTIGONE:
                      Yes, for these hands
of Theseus and his dearest comrades saved us.

OEDIPUS:
Come here, children, to your father! Give me your bodies
to embrace, which have come back beyond all hope!   1105

ANTIGONE:
You shall get what you beg, for we yearn to grant the favor.

---

120. Apollo was god of the bow and Artemis, his sister, was goddess of
hunting.

OEDIPUS:
Where then, where are you both?

ANTIGONE:
                Here we are, approaching together.

(Oedipus and his daughters embrace.)

OEDIPUS:
Dearest offshoots!

ANTIGONE:
                Everything is dear to its parent.

OEDIPUS:
Scepters to support me!

ANTIGONE:
                Ill-fated ones for an ill-fated man.

OEDIPUS:
I have my dearest ones! I would no longer be utterly   1110
miserable if I died, with you two standing by me.
Press your sides, children, to right and left of me,
growing one with him from whom you grew, and stop me
from that desolate unhappy former wandering.
And tell me what was done as briefly as possible, since   1115
little speech suffices for girls your age.

ANTIGONE:
This is the one that saved us. You must hear him, father,
and the deed will be brief for both you and me.

OEDIPUS:
Stranger, be not amazed at my persistence,
if I prolong words to my children, appearing to me beyond hope.   1120
For I understand that this delight of mine in these
girls has appeared to me from none other than you.
It was you who saved them, and no other mortal.
May the gods reward you as I wish,
both you yourself and this land. For I have found   1125
reverence among you alone of human beings,
and equity, and absence of false-speaking lips.
Knowing those qualities, I requite them with these words.
For I have what I have through you, and no other mortal.
Hold out your right hand, lord, so that   1130
I may touch and kiss—if it is permitted—your face.
     Yet what am I saying? How could I, reduced to misery,
want you to touch a man in whom every possible
stain of evil resides? I do not want it,
nor indeed shall I allow it. For only those mortals   1135
experienced in these things can join in suffering them.
Receive my greeting from where you are, and in the future
care for me justly, as you have to this moment today.

THESEUS:
  I am not amazed if you have drawn out your words
  at some length, delighting in these children here,   1140
  nor yet if you chose their words before mine.
  These things do not weigh heavily upon us.
  It is not with words that we endeavor to make
  our life shine, so much as with deeds performed.
  I show this. For in none of what I swore did I play   1145
  you false, old man. Here I am, bringing these girls
  alive, untouched by those threatenings.
  What need to boast in vain of how the struggle
  was won? You will learn it yourself from being with these two.
    But share with me your judgement of the word   1150
  that fell upon my ear just now as I proceeded here.
  It is little in the telling, but worthy of amazement,
  and human beings should dishonor no event.

OEDIPUS:
  What is it, child of Aegeus? Tell me,
  for I myself know nothing of what you inquire about.   1155

THESEUS:
  They say that some man, not your fellow-citizen
  but your kinsman, has somehow fallen suppliant
  and taken up his seat at the altar of Poseidon, just
  where I was sacrificing when I set out.[121]

OEDIPUS:
  Where is he from? What does he desire with his suppliancy?   1160

THESEUS:
  I know one thing only: with you, so they tell me,
  he begs a brief word—not one full of trouble.

OEDIPUS:
  What word? For that suppliant seat is of no little account.

THESEUS:
  With you they say he begs to come and speak,
  and then depart unharmed by his road here.   1165

OEDIPUS:
  Who then could he be, who sits in supplication at this seat?

THESEUS:
  See whether you have any kinsman in
  Argos, who might desire to win this favor from you.

OEDIPUS:
  Dearest friend, stop where you are!

THESEUS:
                        What is it?

OEDIPUS:
  Do not entreat me...

---

121. On suppliancy see Introduction p. 11-12.

THESEUS:
To do what? Tell me!   1170

OEDIPUS:
I know well, hearing this, who the suppliant is.

THESEUS:
Whoever is he then, with whom I am to find fault?

OEDIPUS:
My child, lord, whom I abhor! Whose words of all men
it would give me most distress to endure hearing!

THESEUS:
What? Is it not possible to listen, and not do what   1175
you do not desire? Why is this painful for you to hear?

OEDIPUS:
That voice, lord, has come to be most hateful to his father.
Do not subject me to the necessity of yielding in this.

THESEUS:
But reflect whether his suppliancy exerts necessity—
whether you must guard respect for the god.   1180

ANTIGONE:
Father, be persuaded by me, though I am young to counsel you.
Allow this man to provide the favor
that he wishes to his own mind and the god,
and yield to our plea for our brother to come.
For he will not—have confidence!—wrench you by force   1185
from your own judgement by speaking to your disadvantage.
In hearing words what is the harm? Indeed, evilly
devised deeds are shown up by words.
You begot him. So it is not permitted,
even if he does you the most impious of most evil deeds,   1190
father, for you to do him evil in return.
Allow him to come! Others too have evil offspring
and sharp rage, but when they are advised
by the incantations of friends their nature is charmed.
Reflect not on the present, but on those   1195
paternal and maternal troubles that you suffered.
If you look on them, I know, you will recognize
that evil is the end of evil rage.
You have no slight reasons for such thought,
deprived as you are of your sightless eyes.   1200
Yield to us! For it is no fine thing that those with just
desires should have to be persistent, nor that one should be well
treated and not understand how to repay such treatment.

OEDIPUS:
Child, you conquer me, winning a heavy pleasure

by your words.[122] Let it be, then, as is dear to you.   1205
Only, stranger, if that man comes here,
let no one ever gain power over my life!

THESEUS:
Once do I desire to hear such things, not twice,
old man. I do not wish to boast; but know
that you are safe, if any of the gods keeps me safe too.   1210

(Exit Theseus, in the direction of Colonus.[123])

Strophe [124]

CHORUS:
Whoever desires the greater
portion, neglecting moderation,
for his life, will in my view be shown up
as a guardian of stupidity.
For the long days   1215
lay up many things
closer to pain, nor can you
discern delights,
when someone falls into a longer life
than is needful. But the Helper ends it equally,[125]   1220
when one's share of Hades,[126] without wedding-song,
without lyre, without dance, has appeared—
death at the end.

Antistrophe
Not to be born conquers every
reckoning.[127] But to go, once one has   1225

---

122. The "you" here is plural, referring to both Antigone and Theseus. The "pleasure" that Oedipus grants to them by agreeing to their wishes is "heavy" on himself because he hates his son. Note that this passage proves Creon wrong in his view that Oedipus wants to "conquer" his friends (849-52) (see further Interpretation p. 100).
123. Theseus returns to the altar of Poseidon, to summon Polynices and resume the sacrifice interrupted at 887 (cf. 1491-5). This keeps him conveniently available for a hasty return at 1500.
124. The chorus sing the third *stasimon*, consisting of one strophic pair with an extra stanza or epode (1211-48). The pessimistic mood is in stark contrast to the joy of the first *stasimon* (668-719) and excitement of the second (1044-95), and establishes an ominous mood for Oedipus' encounter with his son.
125. The "Helper" is death, who delivers all alike from life's sufferings.
126. Hades, god of the underworld, stands for death (cf. 1440), as Ares does for war (cf. 1047).
127. This is perhaps the most famous statement of a notoriously pessimistic Greek proverb (see further Interpretation p. 101).

appeared, as quickly as possible
to the place one has come from,[128]
is second best by far.
For when youth is present,[129]
bringing empty thoughtlessness, 1230
what trouble wanders far
away? What hardship is not within?
Envy, factions, strife,
battles and murders!
And the final allotment is 1235
disparaged, powerless, unsociable,
friendless old age, where all
evils of evils reside together.

Epode

Such is the age of this enduring man—not mine alone.
As some north-facing headland, wave-lashed 1240
on all sides, is battered in a storm,
so this man too is battered
over the head by dreadful
dooms breaking like waves, ever his companions,
some from the sinking of the sun, 1245
some from its rising,
some at its midday beam,
some from the night-shrouded Rhipae.[130]

(Enter Polynices, from the direction of Colonus.)

ANTIGONE:
But here is our stranger, so it seems.
He is at least without men, father, and pours 1250
tears from his eyes in streams as he journeys this way.[131]

OEDIPUS:
Who is he?

ANTIGONE:
The one we had in mind
from the first: Polynices—here he is.

POLYNICES:
Alas, what shall I do? Shall I shed tears first
at my own evils, children,[132] or at seeing those of 1255

---

128. That place is the underworld, since humans were sometimes portrayed in myth as born from the earth.
129. Or "when youth has passed."
130. The Rhipae are a mythological mountain range in the far north, imagined as permanently darkened by stormy gloom. The chorus thus cover the four points of the compass.
131. Note the contrast with Creon's entrance (722-3).
132. In Greek, unlike English, this is not an unnatural way to address one's siblings (cf. 1420, 1431).

my old father here?—whom I have found in a strange
land here with you two, an outcast,
in clothing such as this, the unlovely filth of which
has taken up residence, old itself, with this old man,
wasting his sides; and on his head, bereft of eyes,   1260
his hair flutters unkempt in the breeze;
and akin to this, it seems, he carries with him
the nurture of his woeful stomach.[133]

(He turns to address his father directly.)
All this I—ruinous as I am!—learn far too late.
And I attest that I have been the evillest of mortals   1265
in regard to your nurture.[134] Discover what I am from no one else.
But—for even Zeus has sitting with him on his throne
Respect, in all his deeds—by you too, father,
let her stand.[135] For there are remedies
for faults committed, but no increase is possible.   1270

(He pauses, but Oedipus does not reply.)
Why are you silent?
Speak, father, some word! Do not turn away from me!
Have you no response for me? Will you send me away dishonored
by your speechlessness,[136] not even telling the reason for your
                                                    wrath?[137]

(Oedipus remains silent, and Polynices turns back to his sisters.)
Oh this man's seed, and my own sisters,   1275
do *you* at least attempt to move our father's
lips, so hard to approach and to address,
that he may not thus let me go dishonored—a suppliant
of the god—having said not a word in reply.

ANTIGONE:
Say yourself, long-suffering one, the desire that brings you
                                here.   1280
For abundant words, by giving delight

---

133. Oedipus carries a beggar's pouch or wallet to hold the food he has
managed to beg. Note the elaborate, stilted style of this long sentence.
134. Caring for one's parents in old age was enormously important in
Greek society (see Interpretation p 94-5).
135. Polynices personifies *aidos*, "respect," as an attendant of Zeus. On
aidos see above, n. 32 (note that it does not mean "mercy," as it is often
misleadingly translated here). For the personification compare 1381-2
and 1767, with notes.
136. An answer is part of the "honor" due to Polynices as a suppliant, since
his request was to converse with Oedipus (1162, 1164). But both Antigone
and Theseus make it clear that the suppliancy does not oblige Oedipus
to accede to his son's request for help (1175-6, 1185-6).
137. The word translated "wrath" (*menis*) is often used for the wrath of
gods and cult heroes (cf. 965, 1328).

or showing distress or somehow expressing pity,
do produce some speech in the speechless.
POLYNICES:
Then I shall speak out—for you guide me well—
first claiming the god himself as my   1285
defender, from whose altar the king of this land
raised me up to come here, granting me
to speak and listen and depart unharmed.
I wish this promise to be kept to me
by you, strangers, and these two sisters and my father.   1290
  But now I want to tell you, father, why I came.
I have been driven from my fatherland, an exile,
because I thought fit, as my birthright by primogeniture,
to take my seat on your all-ruling throne.[138]
In return for this, Eteocles, who is younger by birth,   1295
thrust me from the land, neither conquering me in argument
nor coming to the test of blows and deeds,
but persuading the city.[139] For these events I say
your Erinys is most probably responsible;[140]
and this is also what I hear from prophets.   1300
So when I came to Dorian Argos,[141]
taking Adrastus as my father-in-law, I established
as my sworn allies all in the land of Apis who are
called preeminent and are honored for the spear,[142]
so that, gathering with these the seven-speared   1305
expedition to Thebes,[143] I might either die in a just cause,
or cast those who did these deeds out of the land.
  Very well. Why then have I now come?
Bringing prayerful entreaties to you, father,
both my own and those of my allies,   1310
who now with seven companies and seven

138. Polynices' claim to the throne is weakened by the fact that primogeniture was not customary in classical Greece (see Introduction p. 17).
139. Polynices suggests that his brother won power by manipulating the people. But the democrats in Sophocles' audience might have approved of Eteocles' methods.
140. On the Erinyes as avenging spirits see Introduction p. 11. Here the reference may be to the ancestral curse on the house of Oedipus, or to his personal curse upon his sons (though Polynices has not actually witnessed such a curse), or both (since the one is manifested through the other).
141. Argos is called Dorian because it is in the Peloponnese (see map of mainland Greece below, p. 88), an area inhabited largely by Dorian Greeks.
142. Apis is a name for the Peloponnese (from a mythical king of that name).
143. Polynices and his six allies, whom he goes on to list, are the famous "seven against Thebes," who attacked Thebes at its seven gates and tried unsuccessfully to put Polynices on the throne.

spears are set in siege round the whole plain of Thebes.
One is spear-hurling Amphiareus, preeminent
in power with the spear, preeminent in reading bird-paths;[144]
the second is the Aetolian offspring of Oeneus,   1315
Tydeus; third is Eteoclus, an Argive by birth;
Talaos his father sent Hippomedon
as the fourth; the fifth, Capaneus, proclaims that he
will devastate the city of Thebes, ravaging it with fire;[145]
sixth Arcadian Parthenopaeus rushes forth,   1320
named for the former virgin who in time
gave birth as his mother—the trusty offspring of Atalanta;[146]
and I, your son, and if not yours, then begotten by
an evil destiny, but at least called yours—
I lead the fearless army of Argos towards Thebes.   1325
    All of us together supplicate you, father,
by these children and your own life, begging you
to yield in your heavy wrath against myself,
as I set out for vengeance on my brother,
who thrust me out and robbed me of my fatherland.   1330
For if anything trustworthy comes from oracles,
they said whichever side you join would have the power.
Now by the springs and gods of our race,[147]
I beg you to be persuaded and to yield, since
I am a beggar and a stranger, and you a stranger;   1335
we have a home by flattering others, both you
and I, having been allotted the same fate.
But that autocrat in the house—woe is me!—
luxuriates in mockery at both of us in common.
If you will stand beside my purpose,   1340
with brief trouble and time I shall scatter him.
And so shall I take you and settle you in your house,
and settle myself, having cast him out by force.
With your will on my side these things are mine
to boast of; without you I lack even the strength to save myself. 1345

CHORUS LEADER:
For the sake of the one who sent him, Oedipus, tell
the man whatever is advantageous, then send him away again.

---

144. Amphiareus was an augur, a prophet who foretold the future by
   observing the flight of birds. He foresaw the death of the seven leaders,
   including himself, in the attack on Thebes.
145. Capaneus was noted for his arrogance, for which he was struck down
   in the battle by a thunderbolt from Zeus.
146. Atalanta, who was raised in the woods by a she-bear, would only
   marry a man who could defeat her in a foot race. By this means she
   postponed marriage until Meilanion defeated her by a ruse. Their son's
   name comes from *parthenos*, which means "virgin."
147. Since fresh water is essential to human life, springs were often
   considered symbolic of the land. They were protected by nymphs.

OEDIPUS:
If, gentlemen, the guardian of this land,
Theseus, had not indeed sent him to me
here, thinking it just that he hear words from me,   1350
never indeed would he have heard my voice.
But as it is he will depart thus dignified, having heard
such things from me as shall never gladden his life.

(He turns to address Polynices.)
For when, most evil one, you had the scepter and the throne
which now your brother has in Thebes,   1355
you yourself drove out your own father here,[148]
and made me citiless, and made me wear these garments
which now you weep to see, when, having come
into the same pain, you meet a fate like mine.
But these things must not be cried for, but endured   1360
by me as long as I live, remembering you as a murderer.
For *you* made me be nurtured in this toil,
you thrust me out; because of *you* I am a vagrant,
begging from others my daily livelihood.
If I had not begotten these two children   1365
as my nurses, I would surely not exist, for all *you* did;
as it is these girls preserve me, these my nurses,
these men, not women, at sharing pain;
but you two were begotten by someone else, not me.
  Therefore fate looks upon you, but not yet   1370
as it will shortly, if indeed those troops are moving
against the city of Thebes. For you shall by no means
overthrow that city, but first you shall fall
defiled with bloodshed, and your brother equally.[149]
Such are the curses I let fly at both of you before,[150]   1375
and now I call on them to come to me as allies,
that you two may think fit to revere your progenitors,
and not dishonor your father because he is blind
who begot two such boys; for these girls did not act so.
Therefore these curses overpower your supplication   1380
and your throne, if Justice named of old indeed
exists, sharing the seat of Zeus by ancient law.[151]

---

148. Previously Oedipus accused his sons of failing to speak out against
the exile (427-30), and blamed Creon for perpetrating it (770). But he
holds Polynices equally responsible, especially for failing to recall him
when he had the opportunity.
149. "Defiled" has a double meaning: the brothers will not only be
bloodied, but tainted by fratricide.
150. Cf. 421-7 and see Introduction p. 17.
151 Justice is often personified as a goddess who carries out the will of
Zeus. Oedipus' words are his response to Polynices' personification of
Respect (1267-8).

Be gone! I spit you from me fatherless,
most evil of evil ones! And take these curses with you,
which I call down upon you: neither to overpower with the
        spear   1385
the land of your own race, nor to return ever
to the valley of Argos, but with kindred hand
to die and kill the one by whom you have been driven out.
Such are my curses! And I call on the loathsome
paternal darkness of Tartarus to give you a new home;[152]   1390
I call on these divinities;[153] I call on Ares,
who has cast into you two this dreadful hatred.
Hear this and proceed! Go and report
to all the Cadmeans, and also to your own
trusty allies, that such are the prerogatives   1395
that Oedipus has distributed to his children.

CHORUS:
Polynices, I take no pleasure in your past
roads; now go back again as quickly as possible.

POLYNICES:
Alas for my path here and my failure!
Alas for my comrades! To what a road's end   1400
have we set out from Argos—woe is me!—
such that I cannot even speak of it
to any of my comrades, or turn back again,
but must meet this fortune speechlessly.
You at least, sisters, children of this man,[154] since   1405
you hear the harsh words of this our father as he curses,
do not, you two, by the gods—if the curses of this
our father are fulfilled, and some home-
coming is yours—do not dishonor me,
but place me in a tomb with funeral offerings.[155]   1410
Then the praise you two win now
from this man for your pains will be joined
by still more, just as great, for serving me.

(Antigone and Ismene cling to Polynices.)

ANTIGONE:
Polynices, I supplicate you, be persuaded by me.

POLYNICES:
In what, dearest Antigone? Speak.   1415

---

152. Tartarus is the part of the underworld where the wicked are punished
for their crimes. The significance of the epithet "paternal" is unclear, but
it may hint at the fact that Oedipus, Polynices' father, is soon to reside in
the underworld.
153. The reference is to the goddesses of the grove (see n. 101).
154. Note the irony of the ambiguous wording, as at 330.
155. Sophocles alludes here to the story dramatized in his earlier play,
Antigone. The dislocated style of this sentence conveys Polynices' despair.

ANTIGONE:
Turn back your army to Argos—as quickly as possible!—
and do not destroy both yourself and the city.
POLYNICES:
But that is impossible. For how could I again
lead the same army, having once shown fear?
ANTIGONE:
What need is there, child, to be enraged again? What   1420
profit comes to you from devastating your fatherland?
POLYNICES:
To be an exile is disgraceful, and for me, the elder,
to be thus laughed at by my brother.
ANTIGONE:
Do you see, then, how you are bringing to pass the prophecies
of this man, who cries out death for both of you from both?   1425
POLYNICES:
Yes, for he wishes it; but I must not give in.
ANTIGONE:
Alas! Woe is me! But who will dare, hearing
the kind of prophecies this man uttered, to follow you?
POLYNICES:
I shall not even report bad news; for a good
general says what is better, not what falls short.   1430
ANTIGONE:
Then are you thus determined on this, child?
POLYNICES:
Yes, and do not restrain me. For my care
will be this road, made ill-destined and evil
by this our father here and his Erinyes.
But may Zeus reward you two well, if you fulfill this for me,[156]   1435
for you will not be able to aid me again, dead or alive.
Let me go now, and farewell! For you will never
again see me living.[157]

(Polynices disengages himself from his sisters' embrace.)
ANTIGONE:
                    Woe is me!
POLYNICES:
Do not bewail me.
ANTIGONE:
                    Who would not weep for you,

---

156. He is repeating his request for burial.
157. The Greek literally means "seeing," an expression often used to mean
"alive" (cf. 1549-50), which touches on the theme of sight and blindness
running through the play.

brother, setting out to a Hades you can foresee?[158]   1440

POLYNICES:
If I must, I shall die.

ANTIGONE:
                   Don't! Be persuaded by me!

POLYNICES:
Do not try to persuade where you must not.

ANTIGONE:
                   Then woe is me indeed,
if I am to be bereft of you!

POLYNICES:
                   These things depend on fate,
to turn out one way or the other. But for you two,
I pray to the gods that you may never encounter evil;   1445
for you are unworthy of misfortune in the eyes of all.

(Exit Polynices, in the direction of Thebes.)

Strophe A [159]

CHORUS:
New evils, I see, have come
anew, new and of heavy destiny,
from the blind stranger—
unless perhaps fate is reaching some goal.   1450
For I cannot call vain
any purpose of divinities.
Time sees, sees all things
always, casting down some things,
and the next day raising others up again.   1455

(A peal of thunder is heard.[160])
The sky roared! Oh Zeus![161]

---

158. As in line 1221, the name of the god Hades stands for death.

159. The chorus now sing two strophic pairs, punctuated by three groups
of five spoken lines from Oedipus and Antigone (1447-99), each of which
has the same symmetrical pattern of line distribution (two lines from
Oedipus, one from Antigone and two more from Oedipus). This dialogue
marks a moment of high tension and leads towards the climax of the
drama.

160. Thunder and lightning were among the signs of Oedipus' end foretold
by Apollo (94-5). The Greek theater did have a device for simulating these
phenomena, but it is uncertain whether it had come into use when this
play was first produced.

161. The chorus appeal to Zeus as the sender of thunder and lightning.
Their cry is echoed in exactly the same position in the antistrophe (1471),
and in a similar place in the second strophe (1485).

OEDIPUS:
Children, children! If anyone is in this place,[162]
would he bring here Theseus, in all ways best of men?

ANTIGONE:
Father, for what purpose are you calling him?

OEDIPUS:
This winged thunder from Zeus will shortly   1460
take me to Hades. Send for him as quickly as possible!

(A second peal is heard.)

Antistrophe A

CHORUS:
See! Again a great roar,
unutterable, cast by Zeus,
crashes down; dread stiffens
the very ends of the hair of my head!   1465
My heart cowers; for in the heavens
a flash of lightning flares again.
What end will it produce?
I dread this; for never does it rush forth
for nothing, nor without fateful outcome.   1470
Oh great sky! Oh Zeus!

OEDIPUS:
Children, the divinely ordained end of this man's
life has come upon him. There is no longer any turning back.

ANTIGONE:
How do you know? From what have you determined this?

OEDIPUS:
I know it well. But someone go as quickly as possible   1475
and fetch me the lord of this country!

(A third peal of thunder is heard.)

Strophe B

CHORUS:
Ah! Ah! See, yet again
the piercing din surrounds us!
Be gracious, divinity,
gracious, if you are indeed bringing   1480
some gloom to the land, our mother.[163]

---

162. Oedipus means anyone besides his daughters and the chorus. His
blindness prevents him from knowing if a suitable messenger is available. In the event, Theseus is not fetched by anyone but arrives in
response to the uproar (1500).

163. According to local legend, the people of Attica were born from the
land. More generally, the earth was the legendary mother of all life,
including the human race.

May I find you propitious,
and may I not, having seen a man accursed,
share somehow in profitless favor.[164]
Lord Zeus, to you I speak!   1485

OEDIPUS:
Is the man near? Will he reach me, children,
still alive and in control of my mind?

ANTIGONE:
What trusty pledge do you want rooted in your mind?

OEDIPUS:
To give them, in return for their good treatment,
fulfillment of the favor that I promised when receiving it.   1490

Antistrophe B

CHORUS:
Oh! Oh! Child, come, come![165]
If at the edge of the hollow,[166]
for Poseidon, god of the sea,
you are indeed hallowing the altar
with sacrifice, come!   1495
For the stranger thinks you worthy,
and your city and your friends,
that he should offer just favor for good treatment.
Hurry, rush, lord!

(Enter Theseus with attendants, from the direction of the village.)

THESEUS:
What uproar resounds again from you in common,   1500
clearly from the citizens, manifestly from the stranger?
Is it at some thunderbolt from Zeus, or some bursting
downpour of hail? For when the god
makes such a storm, one may surmise anything.

OEDIPUS:
Lord, you appeared as I yearned for you. Some god   1505
arranged for you the good fortune of this road.

THESEUS:
What further new event has happened, child of Laius?

OEDIPUS:
The scale of my life is sinking,[167] and I want to die without
playing you and this city false in what I promised.

---

164. The chorus are worried about the nature of the "favor" they will
   receive in return for helping Oedipus (cf. 1498).
165. It is the prerogative of the chorus' age to call Theseus "child," but it
   also suggests affection for their king.
166. The text here is corrupt, but it certainly refers to the location of the
   sacrifice.
167. In the *Iliad* Zeus sometimes holds up a pair of scales to decide a battle
   between two warriors. The side of the one who will die sinks down.

THESEUS:
On what evidence for your doom do you depend?   1510
OEDIPUS:
The gods themselves as heralds are my messengers,
playing me false in none of the appointed signs.
THESEUS:
How are you saying this is made plain, old man?
OEDIPUS:
By the many incessant thunderclaps and many
lightning-flashes from the unconquered hand.   1515
THESEUS:
You persuade me. For I see you making many prophecies
that do not speak false. Say what must be done.
OEDIPUS:
Child of Aegeus, I shall tell you things that will
lie stored up for this city, unpained by old age.
I myself shall shortly guide the way, untouched   1520
by any guide, to the place where I must die.
Never tell this place to any human being—
neither where it is concealed, nor in what region it lies—
that it may always accord you a protection
better than many shields, or neighbors' borrowed spears.   1525
The mysteries, not to be disturbed by words,
you yourself will learn when you go there alone;
for I would not tell them to any of these citizens
or to my children, though I cherish them.
Always keep them safe yourself, and when you come   1530
towards life's end, reveal them to the foremost man
alone; let him show them to his successor, and so on.
And thus will you reside here with your city unravaged
by the sown men.[168] The untold majority of cities,
even if one governs well at home, turn easily to outrage.   1535
For the gods look on late, though well, when
one lets go godliness and turns to frenzy.
Never wish, child of Aegeus, to suffer this yourself.
    Thus far I am informing one who knows.
But to that place—for the god's sign presses me on—
let us now proceed, without further hesitation.

(Oedipus starts to walk , unaided and confident, from the stage.[169])
Children, follow this way. For I have been revealed

---

168. The Thebans are called the "sown men" because in myth their
    ancestors sprang from dragon's teeth sown by Cadmus, the city's founder.
169. There is a powerful dramatic contrast between Oedipus' blind,
    dependent movements until now, and the assurance with which he leads
    the others from the stage, guided by his inner vision.

as a new guide for you, as you two were for your father.
Go onward, and do not touch me, but allo me
myself to find the sacred tomb, where 1545
it is this man's fate to be concelaed in this land.
This way, here, come this way! For this way Hermes
the escort takes me,[170] and the underworld goddess.[171]
Oh light that is gloom to me, once indeed you were mine,
but now my body touches you for the last time.[172] 1550
For I am now moving off to conceal the end
of my life with Hades. But, dearest of strangers,
may you and this country and your attendants
be blessed, and in prosperity
remember me when I am dead, for your good fortune always. 1555

*(Exit Oedipus in the direction of Colonus, followed by his daughters,
Theseus and his retinue.[173])*

Strophe [174]

CHORUS:
If it is permitted for me to revere the unseen
goddess with prayers,[175] and you,
lord of the night-shrouded,
Aidoneus, Aidoneus,[176]
grant me that the stranger 1560
attain neither painfully
nor with a doom of heavy grief
the all-concealing plain

---

170. Hermes was the herald and messenger of the gods. One of his
functions was to escort the souls of the dead to the underworld.
171. Persephone, queen of the underworld.
172. In Greek tragedy dying characters often say farewell to the sunlight
(cf. n. 157). Oedipus has not seen the light since he blinded himself, but
now he feels it on his skin for the last time.
173. Some have thought that Oedipus exits into the grove, since his death
clearly takes place in the vicinity of the shrine. But this would involve a
large number of people, including insignificant attendants, entering the
sacred precinct. Moreover a procession along the *parodos* towards Colonus, led by the newly confident Oedipus, would make an impressive
theatrical contrast with his faltering first entrance from the other side,
guided by Antigone.
174. The chorus sing the fourth and final *stasimon*, consisting of a single
strophic pair (1556-78), which serves as a funeral-song for Oedipus. Like
the second *stasimon* (1044-95), this brief ode represents a considerable
lapse of time (see Interpretation p. 99)
175. The "unseen goddess" is Persephone, queen of the underworld. The
unusual epithet may be explained by the fact that Hades, the name of
her husband and her realm, literally means "unseen" (cf. 1681).
176. Aidoneus is a longer version, sometimes found in poetry, of the name
of Hades, king of the underworld. The chorus address him with some
hesitation, because he is notoriously resistant to prayer.

of the dead below and the Stygian home.[177]
For though many pointless   1565
troubles come upon him,
a just divinity may raise him up again.

Antistrophe

Oh earth goddesses,[178] and unconquered body of the
beast,[179] you who sleep at the gate
that welcomes many strangers,   1570
and whine from your cave,
the untamed guard of Hades,
as the story has always held—
I pray that he, oh child of Earth
and Tartarus,[180] walk clear   1575
of the stranger setting out
to the plains of the underworld.
On you I call, god of everlasting sleep!

(One of Theseus' attendants enters hastily with news, along the parodos
by which Oedipus departed.)

MESSENGER:
    Citizens, I would succeed in speaking
    most concisely if I say that Oedipus has perished.   1580
    But as for what was done, the tale cannot
    be briefly told, nor were the deeds there brief.
CHORUS LEADER:
    He has perished, the unhappy man?
MESSENGER: Understand
    that he has left his life forever.[181]
CHORUS LEADER:
    How? Was it by a godly and painless fortune?   1585
MESSENGER:
    Now this event indeed merits amazement.
    For you too, who were present, know how he moved
    away from here, without any of his friends as guide,
    but he himself serving as guide for all of us.
    But when he had come to the abrupt threshold   1590

---

177. Stygian means "infernal," from the river Styx which runs through
the underworld.
178. The Eumenides, who are underworld or "earth" divinities (see Introduction p. 11).
179. The "beast" is Cerberus, the three-headed dog who guards the
underworld. He was said to fawn on those who entered but devour anyone
who tried to leave.
180. This is probably Death, though in Hesiod he is the child of Night
(*Theogony* 211). On Tartarus, here personified, see n. 152. Death is
certainly the "god of everlasting sleep" invoked at 1578.
181. The text of this line is corrupt, but it certainly refers to Oedipus' end.

rooted in the earth with bronze steps,[182]
he stopped on one of many branching paths,[183]
near the hollow bowl where lies
the ever-trusty pact of Theseus and Peirithous.[184]
Standing midway between this and the Thorician rock,   1595
the hollow pear-tree and the tomb of stone,[185]
he sat down; then he loosed his filthy garments.
Next he called his children, and bade them bring
flowing water for washing and drink-offerings.
The two girls went to the hill of verdant   1600
Demeter which was in view,[186] and in quick time
fetched their father what he ordered, and washed him
and adorned him with clothing, as is customary.[187]
   But when he had had his pleasure of all this activity,
and none of what he desired was left undone,   1605
Zeus of the earth roared,[188] and the maidens
shuddered as they heard. Falling at
their father's knees they cried, and did not slacken from
breast-beating and prolonged lamentation.
When he heard the sudden bitter sound,   1610
he folded his arms round them and said, "Children,
on this day your father no longer exists.
For all my affairs have perished, and you will
no longer have the painful work of nurturing me.
It has been harsh, I know, children. But one word   1615

---

182. See n. 11.
183. These paths converge at the "threshold." The language here recalls
   the famous "branching path" where Oedipus met and killed his father
   (*Oedipus the King* 733).
184. Theseus and his friend Peirithous made a pledge of friendship before
   venturing into the underworld to kidnap Persephone. They were caught,
   but Theseus (and in some versions Peirithous as well) was later rescued
   by Heracles. The place may have been marked by a monumental bowl of
   bronze or stone, or the "bowl" may be a hollow or cave in the rock.
185. The audience would have recognized the significance of these local
   landmarks, which is lost to us. The precise geographical description adds
   to the miraculous effect of the blind man's progress. The actual spot
   where Oedipus disappears must, however, have remained mysterious,
   since its secrecy is so heavily emphasized.
186. Demeter is "verdant" because she is a goddess of vegetation and
   growth. She is also a goddess of the underworld, which makes her an
   appropriate patron for this spot.
187. Preparations for burial of the dead included a ritual washing of the
   corpse and dressing it in white funeral garments.
188. "Zeus of the earth" is a title for Hades, who is supreme in the
   underworld as Zeus is in the sky. Although "roaring" is the word used
   previously for thunder (1456, 1464), it may here signify an earthquake,
   which is more appropriate to the king of the underworld and was
   mentioned by Oedipus as another possible sign of his approaching end
   (95).

alone dissolves all these toils.[189]
For there is no one from whom you have had more
love than from this man, deprived of whom
you will now lead the remainder of your lives."
    Thus did they all cry sobbingly,   1620
clinging to each other. But when they had come
to the end of lamentation, and cries no longer arose,
there was silence. Then a voice suddenly
shouted aloud to him, so that for fear the hair
of all stood upright in sudden dread.[190]   1625
For the god called many times to him in many ways:
"You there! You, Oedipus! What delays us
from going? For your part, you have long been slow!"
When he heard himself being called by the god,
he told Theseus, lord of the land, to come to him.   1630
When he came, Oedipus said, "Dear friend,
give my children your hand's ancient pledge of trust,
and you, children, give yours to this man. Promise
never willingly to betray these girls, and to fulfill all
your future deeds benevolently, for their advantage always."   1635
And he, like a noble man, without lamenting
promised the stranger under oath to do this.
When he had done that, at once Oedipus,
touching his children with blind hands, said,
"Children, you must endure nobly in your minds   1640
and go forth from this region, not thinking it just
to look at what is not permitted, or to hear such speech.
Move away as quickly as possible. Let only Theseus,
who has authority, be present, learning what is done."
    All of us together heard him speaking   1645
thus far. And weeping in streams along with
the maidens, we accompanied them. When we had departed,
after a brief time we turned round, and saw from afar
that man no longer present anywhere,
but just our lord, holding his hand   1650
before his face to shade his eyes, as if some dread
and fearful thing had appeared, unbearable to see.
But then, a little later and after no great time,
we saw him worshiping the earth and Olympus,
home of the gods,[191] both at once in the same prayer.   1655
But by what doom that man perished, not a single
mortal can tell, except Theseus himself.

---

189. The word is "love."
190. The mysterious anonymity of the voice makes it all the more awe-
    some. The god may, however, be identified with Hermes (cf. 1547-8),
    Persephone (cf. 1548 with note), or perhaps Hades himself.
191. "Olympus" here means the sky, home of the heavenly gods, just as
    earth is the home of the gods of the underworld. Theseus is seen bowing
    down to the earth and then immediately raising his arms to the sky, as
    he worships both "earth" and "sky" gods.

For no fire-bearing thunderbolt
from the god destroyed him, nor a tempest,
stirred up at that time from the sea, 1660
but either some escort from the gods, or the earth's unlit
underworld foundation, well-disposed and gaping open.
For the man was not sent away with weeping,
nor distressed by sickness, but amazingly
if ever any mortal was. If my words seem senseless, 1665
I would not try to convince those who think me without sense.

CHORUS LEADER:
Where are the children and their escort of friends?

MESSENGER:
The girls are not far off; for the distinct sounds
of lamentation reveal that they are moving this way.

(Enter Antigone and Ismene, crying aloud, along the parodos *by which
they left.)*[192]

Strophe A

ANTIGONE:
Alas! Woe! It is our lot, it is indeed, 1670
to weep in full for the cursed
blood born in us, ill-fated pair, from our father
for whom we once had
so much unremitting pain;
and now finally we shall declare things beyond reason 1675
that we two saw and suffered.

CHORUS:
What is it?

ANTIGONE:
                        One can but surmise, friends.

CHORUS:
He is gone?

ANTIGONE:
                        In a way you might most yearn for.
Yes indeed! For neither Ares
nor the sea came to meet him, 1680
but the unwatched plains engulfed him,
borne off by some unseen doom.
Woe is me! But for us two, a deadly
night has come upon our eyes.
For how, as vagrants 1685
in some distant land
or on the swell of the sea, shall we obtain
the nurture of a life so hard to bear?

ISMENE:
I do not know. May murderous

---

192. There follow two strophic pairs of highly emotional lyric dialogue
between Antigone, Ismene and the chorus (1670–1750).

Hades overwhelm me, that I may share the death   1690
of my old father—woe is me!—since for me
our future life is unlivable.

CHORUS:
Best pair of children,
do not burn too passionately
at what comes well from the gods;   1695
the way you have fared is no cause for complaint.

Antistrophe A

ANTIGONE:
So there is such a thing as yearning even for evils.
For even what was by no means dear, was dear,
as long as I also had him in my arms.[193]
Oh father! Oh friend![194]   1700
Oh you clad in the everlasting darkness under the earth!
Not even in absence will you ever find
yourself unloved by me and her.

CHORUS:
He did...

ANTIGONE:
      He did as he wanted.

CHORUS:
In what regard?

ANTIGONE:
      In the strange land that he wished, 1705
he died; he has his bed
below well-shaded forever,
and has left behind him cries of mourning.[195]
For these eyes of mine, father, weep
tears for you. Nor can I tell—   1710
woe is me!—how I should
dispel such great sorrow for you.
Alas! You wished to die in a strange land, but
you died thus desolate, without me.

ISMENE:
Oh woe is me! What destiny then[196]   1715
        *   *   *   *
        *   *   *   *

still awaits me and you, friend,

---

193. Antigone means that the sufferings she endured for Oedipus' sake
were outweighed by the pleasure of his company.

194. In Greek the same word (*philos*) means both "friend" and "dear," and
family members are presumed to be one's "friends." It is therefore
perfectly natural to address one's father or sister in this way (cf. 1718,
1725).

195. Not to be mourned was considered a misfortune, for it showed that
one had not been loved in life.

196. Two lines are missing from the text here or nearby.

thus desolate without our father?

CHORUS:
Since he resolved blessedly   1720
the end of his life, friends,
cease from this sorrow. For no one
is beyond the reach of evils.

Strophe B

ANTIGONE:
Back again, friend, let us speed!

ISMENE:
                    To do what?   1725

ANTIGONE:
Longing possesses me...

ISMENE:
               For what? Tell me!

ANTIGONE:
To see the hearth under the earth.[197]

ISMENE:
Of whom?

ANTIGONE:
          Of our father—woe is me!

ISMENE:
But how is that permitted? Don't
you see?

ANTIGONE:
         Why do you rebuke me thus?   1730

ISMENE:
And also...

ANTIGONE:
        What's this yet again?

ISMENE:
... he fell without a tomb, apart from all.

ANTIGONE:
Take me there, then slay me!

ISMENE:
Alas! Woe is me! Where then
so desolate, resourceless, shall I now   1735
live my much-enduring life?

Antistrophe B

CHORUS:
Friends, have no fear.

---

197. Antigone is not referring literally to a hearth, but to her father's grave, his new home under the earth. The hearth both represents the home and is a place where sacrifices are offered, as they would be at a tomb.

ANTIGONE:

But where am I to flee?

CHORUS:

You have both already found a refuge...

ANTIGONE:

What?

CHORUS:

...to prevent your lot from turning out evilly.[198]   1740

ANTIGONE:

I understand.

CHORUS:

What then is in your mind?

ANTIGONE:

How we shall go home
I cannot tell.

CHORUS:

Do not seek it!

ANTIGONE:

Hardship holds us.

CHORUS:

Before it also held you fast.

ANTIGONE:

Intractable then, and now still more extreme!   1745

CHORUS:

You two have indeed been allotted a great sea of troubles.

ANTIGONE:

Woe! Woe! Oh Zeus, where are we to turn?
To what remaining hope
does fate now drive me?   1750

(Enter Theseus with his attendants, along the parodos *by which they left.)*[199]

THESEUS:

Cease your weeping, children. Where
the favor of the earth-gods is laid up in common,[200]

---

198. The chorus are reminding Antigone that she and her sister may remain safely in Athens. She acknowledges their concern (1741), but remains preoccupied with the coming events at Thebes, which she still regards as "home" (1742). The remote possibility of saving her brothers—her last "remaining hope" (1749)—draws her back to her native city (1769-72).

199. The conclusion of the play is in anapaests, a meter of regular rhythm often used for the final lines of a tragedy. Anapaests were recited, like iambic trimeters, rather than sung, but may have had a musical accompaniment.

200. Theseus means that Oedipus' death is a "favor" from the underworld gods both to the dead man himself and to Athens.

one must not mourn; for that brings retribution.

ANTIGONE:
Child of Aegeus, we supplicate you!

THESEUS:
To win what desire, children?   1755

ANTIGONE:
We want to see
for ourselves the grave of our father.

THESEUS:
But it is not permitted to go there.

ANTIGONE:
What did you say, lord, king of Athens?

THESEUS:
Children, that man told me   1760
that no mortal should approach
that region, or speak at
the sacred resting place that is his.
He said that if I performed this well
I would have a country always without pain.   1765
These promises, then, the divinity heard from me,
and all-perceiving Oath, who attends on Zeus.[201]

ANTIGONE:
If these things accord with *his* mind,
they may suffice. But send us
to primeval Thebes, to see if we may   1770
somehow prevent the murder
coming on our brothers.

THESEUS:
I shall do that, and in everything
I do in future, both for your advantage
and to bring favor to the one beneath the earth   1775
who has newly gone, I must not falter.

CHORUS:
Come, cease your weeping
and arouse it no more.
For these events have absolute authority.

*(Exeunt Antigone and Ismene, escorted by some of Theseus' men, in the
direction of Thebes, and all other characters, including the chorus, in
the direction of Colonus and Athens.[202])*

201. The "divinity" is the mysterious power that spoke to Oedipus. The
personified Oath punishes perjury as a servant of Zeus, guardian of oaths
(see Hesiod, *Theogony* 231, *Works and Days* 803-4).
202. This staging accentuates the ominous future of which we have just
been reminded once again (1769-72). Alternatively, Oedipus' daughters
may leave for Athens under Theseus' protection, postponing their departure for Thebes. We have no way of determining the poet's original
intention in this regard.

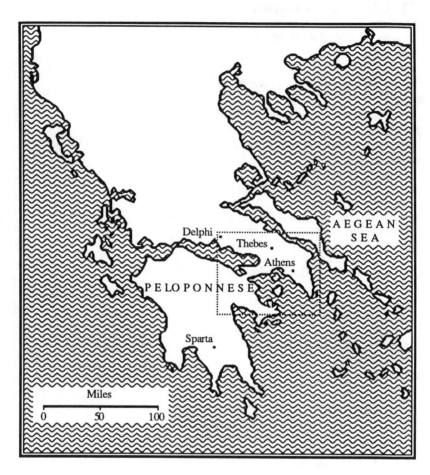

MAINLAND GREECE

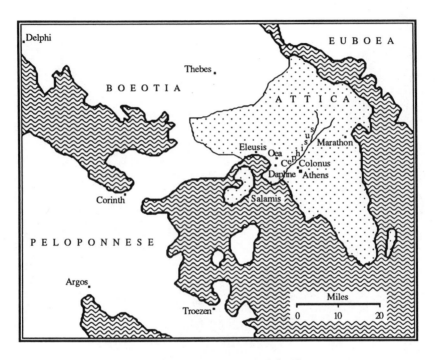

ATTICA AND ENVIRONS

Oedipus at Colonus: An Interpretation

The central action of *Oedipus at Colonus* is framed by the entrance and exit of the awesome figure around whom the drama revolves. As the play opens, the blind, helpless and aged Oedipus is led by his young daughter down one of the long *parodoi* (entrance ramps) towards the shrine of the Eumenides. He will not leave this spot until his climactic departure near the end of the play, when, guided only by his inner vision, he himself leads his daughters and their new friends from the stage. The dramatic effect of this exit, in such striking contrast to Oedipus' entrance, is intensified by the hero's constant presence at his specially chosen location. As he awaits the prophesied moment for his departure, he must face a sequence of visitors, and in doing so overcome various obstacles to the death for which he longs. His uninterrupted presence at the shrine of the Eumenides is emblematic of his determination in face of the various attempts to deflect him by force or persuasion from his goal. As the chorus say, he is like a rock assaulted by wave upon wave of troubles (1240-48), but he remains as unmoved in his purpose as in his location.[1]

The significance of this location is underlined in the opening scene, which not only introduces Oedipus and Antigone and explains their situation, but establishes a powerful sense of place through its repeated references to local landmarks. We should bear in mind that the Athenian acropolis, the most prominent feature of the "towers that shield the city" (14-15), rose up behind the spectators in the theater of Dionysus. Loving geographical detail pervades not only the prologue but the entire play, notably in the

---

1. The play's dramatic structure resembles that of *Prometheus Bound*, a tragedy possibly by Aeschylus, in which the hero remains fixed to a rock throughout the drama. Like Oedipus, Prometheus is a superhuman benefactor who receives a series of visitors at his rock.

stranger's description of Colonus (54-63), the choral ode celebrating Colonus and Attica (668-719), the chorus' speculative account of the battle (1044-73), and the messenger's description of the landmarks near the spot where Oedipus meets his death (1590-1603). This geographical specificity provides the physical and emotional background against which the drama develops, and helps to unify the dramatic events through their local context.

The local environment is rich in religious associations. This applies above all to the drama's actual setting, the sacred grove of the Eumenides, which Antigone lyrically describes for her blind father and ourselves (16-18). It is a place of dread for ordinary mortals like the stranger (39-40) and the chorus (125-32). But Oedipus enjoys a special affinity with this spot and its fearsome occupants. He claims a right to enter the grove as a suppliant of the goddesses, who to him are paradoxically "sweet" (106). This affinity between him and the Eumenides reflects their cultic association in real life (see Introduction p. 14). In the drama it is brought out by numerous similarities in the way they are described. The chorus' reaction to Oedipus as "Dreadful to see! Dreadful to hear!" (141) echoes their response to the goddesses, who are "dread-eyed" (84) and must be passed without a look or a word (128-32; compare also 490). Oedipus' grave must likewise not be looked upon (1641-2, 1652) or addressed (1762-3). Both Oedipus and the goddesses are in a mysterious sense "all-seeing" (42, 74), and both bring their friends the gift of supernatural "kindness" (486-7, 631). Oedipus even underlines his affinity to these goddesses, who do not accept offerings of wine, by saying that he comes "sober" to the "wineless" (100).

Oedipus also shares the double nature of these goddesses, their ability to bless and curse (see Introduction p. 11). Their benign aspect is expressed not only in the benevolent welcome that he receives from them and from Theseus, but also in the blessing he himself bequeaths to Athens. With this blessing is bound up the destruction of his enemies through his curse. The curse, which Polynices calls his father's Erinys or "Fury" (1299, 1434), reflects the goddesses' dark side, their role as avenging Furies, which complements their benevolent aspect as Eumenides or "Kindly Ones". Their destructive potential, emphasized by the nervous chorus at the beginning of the play, is realized in the course of it through the person of Oedipus, their suppliant, who will soon join them as a chthonian or "earth" power, sharing their dual power for vengeance and blessing.

Oedipus thus embodies the ancient code of popular ethics which was based on helping friends and harming enemies and was strongly associated with cult heroes (see Introduction p. 12).[2] The entire play is structured around his overwhelming desire and special power to live up to this moral code. At the outset he reveals Apollo's prophecy, whose fulfillment will constitute the action of the play. He is to find rest at Athens, "bringing profit by residing there to those who welcomed me, but doom to those who sent me away, driving me out" (92-3). The dual theme is restated more explicitly when he tells the chorus that if they help him, "you will gain for this city a great savior, and for my enemies, pain" (459-60). For about the first 700 lines of the play, until the arrival of Creon, Oedipus' two-edged hopes and emerging power to implement them are constantly stressed (e.g. 72-4, 287-8, 401-2, 421-4, 462-3, 576-82, 621-3, 625-8, 642-8). The dramatic action then polarizes the two aspects of this double theme. The fierce hatred with which Oedipus denounces his enemies, Creon and Polynices, is contrasted with the love that unites him and his daughters (see especially 1099-1114). It is only after Polynices' tragic exit that the emphasis shifts exclusively to the benign aspect of Oedipus' power, which dominates the final portion of the play (see 1488-90, 1496-8, 1508-9, 1518-55).

After Oedipus takes refuge at the shrine, a whole series of characters come to visit him there. The dramatic impact of these scenes is diverse and at the same time cumulative. The poet skillfully varies the manner in which each new arrival is introduced, and makes a different dramatic point in each case, yet uses them all to propel the action towards a single goal. The tone is varied from scene to scene, from the joyful excitement of Ismene's arrival, to the lively kidnapping and rescue at the center of the play (which help to prevent the plot from becoming static), to the appalling ferocity of Oedipus' final denunciation of his son and the tragic pathos of Polynices' departure. The emotional force of each encounter tops the previous one, culminating in the scene with Polynices. Even this is outdone, however, by the extraordinary ending, which tells us of Oedipus' ultimate encounter, with the gods of the underworld and death itself. This is the climax of the theatrical crescendo which accompanies the steady increase in Oedipus' heroic powers.

2. For a fuller discussion of this code and its significance in the play see ch. 2 and 7 of my book, *Helping Friends and Harming Enemies* (Cambridge 1989), from which much of this essay is drawn.

Oedipus' first visitor is a minor character, the stranger who arrives to investigate the new arrivals and leaves to report their presence to the local authorities. His dramatic function is to provide both characters and audience with information about the setting, and then leave Oedipus free to invoke the goddesses of the grove (84-110). This solemn and impressive prayer explains the significance of Oedipus' arrival at the shrine, and creates a sense of awe and anticipation at the opening of the drama. (Note especially the prophesied signs of Oedipus' approaching death (94-5), which will be fulfilled at the end of the play.) As Oedipus finishes his prayer, the chorus arrive. They are noblemen, Athenian citizens and residents of Colonus, who illustrate the reaction of ordinary people to the polluted Oedipus. They are pious and well meaning, yet they are overcome with such horror that they break their promise of sanctuary (226-36; contrast 176-7). This behavior is prompted by a kind of piety, for Oedipus is tainted by religious pollution and the chorus fear the wrath of the gods (234-6). But the chorus' piety leads them to violate not only the moral obligation to keep a promise, but the religious obligation to shield a suppliant (see Introduction p. 11-12). They claim that this violation is justified by the principle of retaliatory justice, which permits the reciprocation of one "deceit" for another (228-32). But Oedipus can scarcely be said to have deceived them, and even if he had, it is not clear that this would justify their behavior. The dramatic point of the broken promise is both to leave some uncertainty as to Oedipus' safety, thus generating suspense (compare 802-3, 822), and to express as powerfully as possible the horror that he inspires. The fundamental decency and restraint of the chorus are shown, however, by their pity (254-5, 461-2) and their willingness to listen to persuasion and submit the matter to a higher authority (292-5).

The next arrival is Ismene, whose reunion with her father and sister gives rise to a touching display of familial love. Her news from Thebes makes an important contribution to Oedipus' growing understanding of his destiny, and puts both him and ourselves in a position to evaluate the subsequent overtures of Creon and Polynices. The poet has also ingeniously developed Ismene's role so as to provide Oedipus with a pair of loving and nurturing daughters in contrast to his two delinquent sons—a contrast most colorfully expressed through the alleged parallel with the Egyptians (337-45). The obligation to care for one's parents in their old age was one of the most powerful moral imperatives of Greek society (in classical Athens it was mandated by law). It was construed as reciprocation for the nurturing of children by their parents—hence the emphasis throughout the play on the "nurture" of Oedipus. Oedipus' daughters have fulfilled this obligation at considerable personal cost, whereas his sons, upon whom such obligations primarily fell (since the responsibilities of women in Greek society were severely limited), have completely neglected it.

In his passionate denunciations of his sons, Oedipus has aptly been compared to Shakespeare's Lear. But this hatred is offset by the affection that unites him with his daughters. Their mutual love is emphasized throughout the play, especially at Ismene's arrival, after the rescue of the kidnapped girls, and at Oedipus' death. These scenes make it clear that Oedipus is far from deficient in natural love for those children who behave as children ought. This is confirmed by his parting words to them (1615-19), and by their extravagant grief at his death. As Antigone puts it, "everything is dear to its parent" (1108). This line is highly ironic in view of the forthcoming confrontation between Oedipus and Polynices, but it serves to underline the natural state of family relations which has been perverted by the sons' behavior.

The chorus respond with pity and concern to Oedipus' tirade against his sons, and are impressed by his promise of protection to Athens (461-4). They therefore explain the purifying rites necessary to propitiate the goddesses for intruding into their grove (466-92). This detailed description is a substitute for the dramatization of the rites, and symbolizes Oedipus' reconciliation with the gods. It is not strictly a purifying rite for the pollution of his past deeds (such rites would presumably have been carried out as soon as possible). But in dramatic terms the emphasis on purity and reconciliation fulfills this function. Ismene departs into the grove to perform the ritual, and meanwhile the chorus interrogate Oedipus about his past (510-48). Once again they represent the reactions of ordinary mortals. Their curiosity about Oedipus' deeds may seem tactless and even prurient, but it is altogether human. In dramatic terms it prepares for a pointed contrast with Theseus, who is about to manifest an utterly different kind of reaction to the polluted stranger.

Theseus comes straight to meet Oedipus and immediately offers to help him, not only out of pity (556), but from personal sympathy with his sufferings and an understanding of the transience of human life (560-8). Although we shall later discover that he has a proper respect for supplication, his initial offer of assistance is made without reference to religious constraints. Only later does he mention Oedipus' suppliant status (634), along with an alliance between Thebes and Athens (632-3), and Oedipus' offer of recompense (635). The practical benefit that goes hand in hand with principle is not to be scorned, for as Oedipus himself puts it, "What good man is not his own friend?" (309). It is clear that this benefit is not Theseus' sole motive, for he must still be persuaded that it is not more "fine" for Oedipus to return to Thebes (590). But the Greeks were quite realistic in their recognition that human decisions and actions are prompted by a multiplicity of motives, and that self-interest and principle are not mutually exclusive. Theseus acts from a confluence of sympathy, piety, loyalty, self-interest and the interests of his city.

For all these reasons, then, he promises to protect Oedipus and make him a resident of the city of Athens (637). He thus reverses Oedipus' status as "citiless" (207, 1357), and provides him with new friends with whose help he can reject the advances of his former friends at Thebes. In return for this "favor" (586), Oedipus will bequeath to Athens a unique "favor" of his own (636, 1490, 1498)— the paradoxical "gift" of his ravaged body (576-7). "Favor" is a key word in the play, and the Greek word (*charis*) has reciprocal connotations. A *charis* is both the favor one offers to another, and the gratitude or reciprocal favor one expects in return (cf. 230-32). It is the exchange of such "favors" that seals the new friendship between Oedipus and Athens (cf. 1752, 1775). Creon, by contrast, is incapable of showing his friendship by bestowing true favor upon Oedipus (779).

The moment of Oedipus' acceptance into Athens is marked by the exquisite and justly famous ode in praise of Colonus and Attica (668-719). This is the play's first *stasimon* (song "in position"), sung and danced by the chorus alone, in contrast to the frantic exchanges of their previous lyric dialogues with Oedipus and Antigone. The song, suffused as it is with love of the land and local religious feeling, not only celebrates Oedipus' new status but provides a moment of joy, serenity, and confidence in the favor of the gods. This mood is abruptly challenged, however, by the entrance of Creon with his armed guard. Creon's overtures have already been undercut by Ismene, who makes clear both that his motives for seeking out Oedipus are entirely self-interested, and that he has no intention of reinstalling his brother-in-law in Thebes itself (396-408). We can therefore enjoy the elaborate hypocrisy and rhetorical artifice of his opening speech from a vantage point of superior knowledge (728-60).

Oedipus answers with a withering attack on Creon's hypocrisy (761-99), and the two angry old men descend to bitter abuse, until Creon finally turns to violence. Oedipus' estimate of his enemy is fully justified when Creon drops his facade of concern and shows his disregard for piety by using brutal force against helpless suppliants. His claim to have justice on his side in abducting Antigone (832) is most implausible. (How could an uncle have a greater claim on her than her father?) He even admits that his behavior is an outrage (*hybris*) (883), and acts rashly against his own better judgement, ignoring the limitations of his age (874-5, 953-5, 958-9; contrast 732-4). He thus embodies the same kind of thoughtless rage of which he accuses Oedipus (804-5, 852-5), and which is deprecated by the calm Theseus (658-60). Yet he suggests that he is a better judge than Oedipus as to where the latter's best interests lie (800-801, 852-5). But the only benefit Oedipus now needs or desires is to attain his fated end among his new friends in Athens. By staying there he will obtain exactly what he wants: revenge on his enemies, blessing for his friends, and an end to his sufferings through a miraculous death that confirms his heroic powers. It would be hard to find a "better" outcome for Oedipus than the one he has chosen for himself. Creon is on potentially stronger ground with his appeal to the wishes and interests of the rest of the Thebans (737-8, 741-2, 759-60). But Oedipus' alienation extends to the city as a whole, from which he was exiled against his will (440-41). It is therefore debatable how far he retains any obligations towards his birthplace. Moreover Polynices will attack regardless; so by helping the incumbent rulers Oedipus would not be saving the city itself from civil war. Disastrous though his wrath will be for its immediate victims, it will not harm his true friends or even increase Theban suffering in the coming war.

The chorus raise an outcry at the kidnapping (884-6), and Theseus returns in response to the uproar. He moves swiftly into action (897-904), proving that he will stand by his promises to Oedipus, even at the risk of his own life (1038-41). He sternly condemns Creon as unjust and lawless (911-16), confirming with the calm voice of reason Oedipus' passionate condemnation of his enemy. Creon defends his actions by invoking the principle of retaliation, claiming to have carried out the kidnapping in response to Oedipus' curses on himself and his family (951-3). The justice of retaliation, which was widely accepted in Greek popular thought, underlies Oedipus' curses on his enemies, and even Theseus, the moral conscience of the play, subscribes to it. But he does so only in the strictest and most limited sense. For he eschews the impulses of anger, and refrains from punishing Creon except by detaining him until the kidnapped girls are restored (904-8). Creon, by contrast, goes beyond the principle of strict repayment in kind by answering Oedipus' words with violent deeds. He is also inconsistent in claiming the right to retaliate when he will not allow it to Oedipus himself. Moreover, and most significantly, Oedipus' curses are themselves a response to Creon's deeds, constituting the only weapons at the blind old man's disposal (cf. 872-3). He did not formally curse Creon and his family (868-70) until *after* his daughters had been kidnapped (818-47) and *after* Creon had threatened Oedipus himself with violence (860-61). So Creon's claim to the justice of retaliation is suspect on many counts.

The second main element in Creon's self-defense is his appeal to the Areopagus (947-9), an ancient court at Athens which had special jurisdiction over murder and religious pollution. It met on a rocky hill near the acropolis, which was also the location of the Athenian cult of the "Solemn Ones," or Eumenides, and the Athenian hero-cult of Oedipus himself. (Aeschylus' play *Eumenides* dramatizes the installation of the goddesses in this spot.) In invoking the Areopagus, Creon is claiming that a polluted man should under no circumstances receive sanctuary. He is ascribing to Athens the kind of piety that prompted the chorus to break their initial promise to Oedipus. But we have by now seen a more enlightened and humane conception of piety from Theseus, for whom the obligation to protect a suppliant takes precedence over the potential risk of sheltering a polluted man. As the city's authoritative mouthpiece, he makes clear that Creon was mistaken in his assumptions about Athenian piety. This is consistent with other tales in which Athens accepted polluted killers, not just morally innocent ones like Oedipus and Heracles, but deliberate murderers such as Orestes and even Medea.[3]

Oedipus reacts to Creon's mention of his terrible past by launching into a sustained defense of his own innocence (960-1002). This is the third and longest self-defense that he offers in the course of the play (cf. 265-74, 521-48). He argues that he performed his terrible deeds in ignorance and, in the case of his father's murder, in self-defense, making a powerful case for the primacy of moral innocence over religious taint. He does not deny his pollution, as we shall see when he refuses to touch Theseus

---

3. Aeschylus' *Eumenides* dramatizes the Athenian acceptance of Orestes, who killed his mother Clytemnestra at the command of Apollo. For Heracles, who killed his children in a fit of madness, and Medea, who killed hers in cold blood, see Euripides' *Heracles* and *Medea* respectively. In *Heracles* Theseus plays a welcoming role similar to his role in *Oedipus at Colonus* (compare especially his reaction to Heracles' pollution at 1398-1400.)

(1130-36). But he does deny most vehemently that it justifies treating him as a guilty man. This view is confirmed by the behavior of Theseus, that paragon of enlightened piety and virtue, who does not even need to hear Oedipus' self-defense in order to treat him with compassion and respect. He shows so little fear of pollution that he is even willing to welcome Oedipus under his own roof (643).

When Creon has been silenced by Oedipus' denunciation, Theseus turns to the task of proving his good faith by rescuing the girls. The rescue is portrayed by means of a choral ode, in which the chorus speculate imaginatively on the course of the battle as it takes place (1044-95). Their song provides a dramatic substitute for the staging or direct reporting of the battle, enabling the poet both to compress this part of the plot and to reserve the climactic device of a messenger speech for the end of the play. Choral song is often used like this to manipulate dramatic time. The shift of attention to the song and dance of choral performance, together with the accompanying pause in the stage action, makes it easy for the audience to accept that a considerable period of time has passed—in this case, long enough for the pursuit of Oedipus' daughters (which, at least in the choral imagination, is extensive), followed by a lively battle and the victors' return. We shall see a similar use of choral song near the end of the play, where the short fourth stasimon (1556-78) represents sufficient time for all the events reported by the messenger to take place.

The reunion of Oedipus with his daughters, like the moment of Ismene's arrival, illustrates the love that unites at least these members of the family. It also varies the dramatic mood, after the fury of Oedipus' confrontation with Creon and the activity and excitement of the kidnapping, and prior to Oedipus' ominous encounter with Polynices. The announcement of the latter's arrival casts an immediate pall over Oedipus, for whom even his son's voice is "most hateful to his father" (1177). The converse of the delight he takes in the company of his daughters is his intense revulsion from the presence of his son. But Theseus and Antigone succeed in persuading him to receive Polynices. Theseus appeals to piety, which demands respect for supplication (1179-80). This is a crucial virtue for Oedipus, who is not only a suppliant himself, but emphasizes his own sacred status (287), believes that the gods are on his side (e.g. 621-3, 1380-82), and insists that they reward the pious and punish the impious (278-81).

Antigone adds to Theseus' brief reproof her own eloquent appeal. She has already exerted a moderating influence in the prologue, advising Oedipus to conform to local custom (170-2), and acting as a tactful intermediary between him and the chorus (213-18, 237-53). Later she will also mediate between Oedipus and Polynices (1280-83), and try to prevent her brother's fatal enterprise (1414-46). Now she supplements Theseus' religious argument with an appeal to reciprocal favor (*charis*), begging Oedipus to grant Theseus' request as a favor to him as well as to the god (1182-3; cf. 1202-3). She is the one person in the play—and one of very few in the whole of Greek literature—who denies a father's right to retaliate against his son (1189-91). Most Greeks counted maltreatment of a father by his son among the most heinous of offences, and one against which revenge is fully justified. But Antigone, like her counterpart in Sophocles' earlier play, treats the bond of kinship as inalienable.

Although Oedipus will ultimately reject Antigone's argument, her speech, together with Theseus' words, achieves its immediate purpose. Her father capitulates without a murmur, making his point with an oxymoron: the "pleasure" he grants his friends is "heavy" or burdensome to himself (1204). This openness to persuasion is important for Oedipus' character. It enhances his moral stature and enables him to maintain his ethical consistency. For by agreeing to see Polynices he lives up to the respect for suppliancy and belief in the reciprocity of favors which are fundamental to his own claim to protection from Athens. He also shows that he is willing, when necessary, to sacrifice his own pleasure to that of his friends—the kind of sacrifice he himself expects both from his daughters, who have endured considerable hardship for his well-being, and from Theseus, who risks his life to save the girls. The favor that Oedipus agrees to may seem a slight one, but it is represented as extremely painful to him (1169-78). His acquiescence, with the words "you conquer me" (1204), shows that Creon was wrong to accuse him of wishing to "conquer" his friends by pursuing his own desires regardless of theirs (852-5). It also means that when he rejects Polynices we cannot attribute this merely to a stubborn unwillingness to listen to persuasion.

As we await Polynices' arrival the chorus sing the third *stasimon*, on the evils of old age (1211-48). This song develops the mood of foreboding established by Oedipus' reluctance to see his son. In it the old men of Colonus lament the sufferings of the aged, which afflict both themselves and above all Oedipus, with whom they are united by a bond of sympathy (1239). The first antistrophe opens with a famous statement of pessimism about the human condition: "not to be born conquers every reckoning" (1224-5). This sentiment reflects a piece of Greek proverbial wisdom. It should not, however, be taken as a general statement of faith by Sophocles or the Greeks generally. Many writers convey a very different attitude towards human life (compare Sophocles' own ode in praise of human achievements at *Antigone* 332-75), and some explicitly challenge this piece of folk wisdom. The ode as a whole, including this sentiment, must be read in its dramatic context. It does indeed offer a deeply pessimistic view of the human condition. But the circumstances of Oedipus' life, and in particular his relationship with his son, have given the chorus every reason for pessimism.

Against this gloomy background Polynices makes his entrance. After Creon's lies and violence, he represents a challenge of a different kind. In marked contrast to Creon, he arrives weeping and alone (1250-51). His opening words express tearful repentance, and he goes on to beg forgiveness and promise restitution (1254-70; cf. 1342). Unlike the hypocritical Creon, he admits that he has been "the evillest of humans" towards his father (1265-6; contrast 743-4), and confesses the significance of the oracle (1331-2). We are given no reason to doubt his sincerity. Moreover his suppliancy places him in the same position as Oedipus himself. Like Oedipus and Antigone in the first part of the play, he pleads both for "respect" (*aidos*) (1267-8; cf. 247), and for the "honor" that is the suppliant's due (1273-4, 1278-9; cf. 285-6). In recalling their shared experience of exile (1335-7), he even echoes the grounds on which Theseus offered his friendship (562-6).

Oedipus is unrelenting, but finally agrees to answer his son for Theseus' sake (1346-51). The irony here is that only by speaking, and thus "honoring" the suppliant, does he finally seal Polynices' fate. He disowns his son and condemns him as "most evil of evil ones" (1383-4), announcing that he will always consider him a murderer (1361), and cursing him in turn with death (1385-8). He resists both Antigone's moving plea against vengeance on one's children, and Polynices' own attempt at reconciliation. How far is this horrifying intransigence justified? Critics have been divided on the question. Forgiveness per se is not a characteristically Greek virtue, but Polynices' repentance and promised restitution should not be rejected out of hand. The compensation he offers, however, is both inadequate and inextricable from his own self-interest. Still more important, the time for it has passed. Oedipus has already found new friends and the fated resting place for which he longs. There is nothing left that his son can do for him. Polynices speaks truly when he laments that he learns of his father's misery "far too late" (1264). Moreover his appeal to the shared experience of exile is specious (and tactlessly expressed, when at 1336 he speaks of Oedipus as "flattering" his Athenian hosts). Unlike Theseus, Polynices owed his father sympathy from the start, but has only come to sympathize with his condition now that he is forced to share it, as Oedipus affirms in his tirade (1354-9). Rather than a legitimate ground for reconciliation, Polynices' exile is a just retribution for reducing his father to such straits.

But what of the simple fact of family ties? In rejecting the claims of kinship from a delinquent son, Oedipus has popular Greek sentiment on his side, for the greatest possible opprobrium was reserved for children who mistreated their parents. Polynices' failure in this regard is underlined in dramatic terms by the position of the ode on the miseries of old age, which comes just before his entrance. But Antigone's speech suggests that popular morality may be open to criticism on this point. We cannot therefore reject kinship out of hand as a reason for forgiveness. But in the house of Oedipus, any appeal to kinship is a two-edged sword. Not only is it precisely against the obligations of kinship that Polynices has offended, but if Oedipus were to relent and forgive one son, he would still be condemning Thebes to civil war and his other son to death. There is no indication that Eteocles deserves this any more than his brother. (The only disparagement of Eteocles comes at 1338-9 from Polynices, who is scarcely disinterested.) The brothers, like their sisters, are consistently treated as a pair, who are similar in behavior and equal in responsibility. No reason at all is given why Oedipus should take Polynices' side against Eteocles. Polynices represents both brothers, and both are equally damned. Moreover Oedipus' resistance is ultimately constructive, for it is this which enables him to leave his tomb as a protection for his new friends, who have proved their moral worth. Oedipus' revenge on his sons is therefore just. But it is also frighteningly harsh. With his climactic curse he becomes the mouthpiece of his own Erinyes, the unforgiving goddesses of curses and retribution who constitute the dark side of the benevolent Eumenides.

The epilogue to Polynices' encounter with his father, in which Antigone tries to dissuade him in turn from his chosen course, is the final vindication of Oedipus' decision. For having failed to make Oedipus abandon his wrath, Polynices is unwilling to abandon his own. He remains bent on destruction, either of his brother and the Theban army or of himself and his allies. The detailed listing of these allies (1313-22) gives them a reality which makes not only Oedipus' curse but also Polynices' final decision the more terrible.

He is willing to sacrifice their lives as well as his own, in order to avoid disgrace and mockery (1422-3). This emphasis on honor, rather than the practical benefits of his enterprise, underlines the destructive futility of Polynices' decision. Although he is a pathetic, even a tragic figure, he is as intransigent as Oedipus himself, rejecting any solution other than the violent one on which he has determined.

The language of Oedipus' curse on his son's undertaking recalls his own offence against kindred blood (compare 1386 with 407). But Oedipus' deeds, as he so often reminds us, were involuntary, unlike Polynices' willful neglect of his father. Polynices must likewise bear full responsibility for the violence against his brother and his native Thebes. For Oedipus' curse is contingent on Polynices' attempt (1370-72). As Antigone tells her brother, he is bringing the curse upon himself (1424-5). One function of their touching farewell scene is to arouse our sympathy for Polynices, especially by the affection he displays for his sisters (1415, 1444-6). But it also demonstrates unequivocally that he, as well as Oedipus, is responsible for his fate. And finally, it points forward in legendary time to the story of Sophocles' earlier play *Antigone*. When Polynices begs his sisters to be sure to bury him (1405-13, 1435), the audience would naturally remember what happened to Antigone when she carried out this wish. Between them, Oedipus and Polynices by their intransigent anger will unwittingly cause the destruction of one they both dearly love.

With the departure of Polynices the drama moves rapidly towards its final climax. The chorus, filled with a puzzled foreboding (1447-55), are startled by the first of several thunderclaps (1456). This is the moment towards which the whole drama has been moving, when the present starts to come together with the past. We have heard repeatedly of the events long ago which reduced Oedipus to his present condition, and of the more recent prophecies which promised to end it. Past and future finally converge, with the thunder sent by Zeus as a sign that the oracles are on the point of fulfillment (cf. 94-5). All that remains is for Theseus to reappear, so that Oedipus can guide him to the secret spot which will guarantee Athenian victory over Thebes (cf. 621-3). Oedipus speaks of this gift in his last words, every one of which bears weight: "may you... be blessed, and in prosperity remember me when I am dead, for your good fortune always" (1553-5). The verbal arrangement of these lines reflects the inextricable link between proper reverence for the dead Oedipus, and Athenian prosperity. His final word, "always," underlines the permanence of this legacy to Athens.

The blind man's confident departure from the stage, under the mysterious guidance of the gods, represents in compelling theatrical terms the transformation of his fortunes. He first enters as a helpless and pathetic figure, dependent on a young girl and vulnerable to every kind of threat. This helplessness is underlined by his need for guidance at every step (146-8, 173-201), and reiterated in the kidnapping scene and throughout the play (e.g. 495-6, 500-502, 652-6, 1206-7). His blindness is also recalled by subtle touches in the dialogue which emphasize his reliance on sound (e.g. 323, 863, 891, 1177, 1457). Yet Oedipus assures the stranger in the prologue that his prophetic words "will all be seeing" (74). At the dramatic climax this inner vision manifests itself in his assured progress from the stage, in powerful contrast to his previous blind hesitancy. His departure along the other *parodos* from that by which he entered emphasizes visually the transformation of the wretched outcast from Thebes into the savior of Athens.

Oedipus departs to his death, followed by everyone but the chorus, who are left alone on stage to sing the fourth and final *stasimon* (1556-78). This short ode fulfills the function of a funeral-song for Oedipus, as the chorus pray that he may die and reach the underworld without pain. It also represents, like the second *stasimon* (1044-95), a considerable lapse of dramatic time. For the messenger returns at once to give an extensive account of Oedipus' end and the events leading up to it. He starts his narrative in the leisurely fashion typical of tragic messengers, including a detailed account of the spot to which Oedipus led the company (1590-97). This geographical detail not only sustains the sense of place that pervades the entire drama, but makes Oedipus' inner vision more extraordinary by its precision, and gives concrete specificity to the miraculous events that are to follow.

Next we hear how Oedipus, with his daughters' help, prepared himself for death with the rites customarily performed at funerals: drink offerings, ritual washing, and dressing in funeral garments (1598-1603). The daughters mourn their father with "breast-beating and prolonged lamentation" (1609), as was customary for the female relatives of the deceased. In response, Oedipus emphasizes the love that has united the three of them (1615-19), thus helping to dispel the harsh memory of his treatment of Polynices. Father and daughters are permitted to satisfy their desire for lamentation to the full (1620-23). Only then does some mysterious god—perhaps Hermes or one of the underworld divinities—shatter the silence by calling out to Oedipus by name. The shock of this direct address is somehow enhanced by the colloquial intimacy of its style (1627-8). Oedipus responds by commending his daughters to Theseus' care and making a last farewell (1629-44), before proceeding to a death that is left utterly mysterious to all but Theseus (1656-7).

Oedipus' miraculous death is "amazing" (1664; cf. 1586), but it is not the gateway to a blissful hereafter. Like cult heroes generally, Oedipus is mortal, and throughout the play the finality of death is emphasized (e.g. 1220-23). He himself longs for death not as a glorious future, but as a terminus and respite from his sufferings (see especially 84-110). To look on his story as a drama of guilt, atonement and eternal reward is to view it through anachronistic Christian eyes. When the chorus say Oedipus has ended his life "blessedly" (1720), the "blessing" is that he has died, and done so without pain. In Theseus' words, he is one of those for whom death itself is a "favor" (1751-3). Nevertheless, while Oedipus' fate may be no Christian heaven, the gods who caused his downfall have in some sense raised him up (cf. 394, 1453-5, 1565-7), not only by granting him a miraculous and painless death, but by enabling him to help his friends and harm his enemies from beyond the grave. Despite his mysterious disappearance, the audience would think of him, like other cult heroes, as somehow still present under the earth at the spot where he died, and as highly sensitive to the behavior of his friends and enemies. The gods have compensated him in their own inexplicable way, by giving him a demonic power that in many ways resembles their own. His wrath, like theirs, is harsh, unforgiving and effective. Above all, as we have seen (above p. 14, 86), he resembles the Eumenides, the divinities with whose cult he was historically associated, and whose shrine provides the physical and religious setting for this drama.

The extreme grief displayed by Antigone and Ismene on their return demonstrates the bond of true love that united them with their father. In this final scene Antigone shows the same impetuosity and utter devotion to a beloved relative that leads her to her death in *Antigone*. The contrasting characters of the two sisters, as they appear in the previous play, are also sketched here: the more prudent Ismene tries to restrain Antigone, who shows touches of impatience at her sister (1725-33). With the return of Theseus, however, their excited lyrics give way to the more sober and regular anapaestic meter in which the play concludes. Once again Theseus exerts a benignly rational influence. He restrains the sisters' mourning, emphasizing that their father's death is ultimately a "favor" to the dead man himself as well as to Athens (1751-3), and convincing Antigone that she should adhere to Oedipus' dying wishes (1760-69). In accordance with his promise to do all he can for them (1631-7), he agrees to send them back to Thebes in an effort to prevent the future bloodshed between their brothers (1769-76). Ironically, this loyal concern for Antigone's wishes will ultimately lead to her death. Despite Oedipus' efforts to ensure his daughters' future welfare, and despite Theseus' good will, the curse that destroys the sons of Oedipus will also indirectly cause Antigone's ruin. This tragic fact escapes even Oedipus, with his heroic status and prophetic vision of the future.

Suggestions for Further Reading

This is only a tiny sample of the innumerable works devoted to Greek tragedy, Sophocles and *Oedipus at Colonus*. They have been chosen for their interest and accessibility to the English-speaking reader.

Cultural and religious background

Burkert, W. *Greek Religion* (Eng. trans. Cambridge, Mass. 1985) [a comprehensive introduction to the subject]

Dodds, E.R. "On misunderstanding the *Oedipus Rex*," *Greece and Rome* 13 (1966) 37-49; reprinted in E.R. Dodds, *The Ancient Concept of Progress* (Oxford 1973) and E. Segal (ed.) *Greek Tragedy* (New York 1983) [useful on guilt and pollution]

Ehrenberg, V. *From Solon to Socrates* (2nd ed. London 1973) [history of the sixth and fifth centuries with a cultural emphasis]

Books on Greek tragedy

Buxton, R.G.A. *Persuasion in Greek Tragedy* (Cambridge 1982) [includes a discussion of *Oedipus at Colonus*]

Goldhill, S. *Reading Greek Tragedy* (Cambridge 1986) [an introduction from the perspective of contemporary critical theory]

Jones, John. *On Aristotle and Greek Tragedy* (London 1962) [challenges the view that character is central to Greek tragedy]

Kitto, H.D.F. *Greek Tragedy* (3rd ed. London 1961) [a valuable introduction]

Lesky, A. *Greek Tragic Poetry* (Eng. trans. New Haven 1983) [a thorough survey of tragedy and scholarship]

Taplin, O. *Greek Tragedy in Action* (London 1978) [a fine introduction to tragedy in performance]

Vickers, B. *Towards Greek Tragedy* (London 1973) [makes good use of mythic, social and religious background]

Books on Sophocles (all include some discussion of *Oedipus at Colonus*)

Blundell, M.W. *Helping Friends and Harming Enemies: A Study in Sophocles and Greek Ethics* (Cambridge 1989) [discusses Sophocles in the context of Greek popular morality]

Bowra, C.M. *Sophoclean Tragedy* (Oxford 1944) [old-fashioned but still valuable for its learning]

Burton, R.W.B. *The Chorus in Sophocles' Tragedies* (Oxford 1980) [a detailed account of the role of the chorus]

Gardiner, C.P. *The Sophoclean Chorus: A Study of Character and Function* (Iowa City 1987) [looks at the chorus as a character]

Gellie, G.H. *Sophocles: A Reading* (Melbourne 1972) [an accessible introduction]

Kirkwood, G.M. *A Study of Sophoclean Drama* (Ithaca 1958) [good on character and aspects of dramatic technique]

Knox, B.M.W. *The Heroic Temper* (Berkeley 1964) [influential and readable account of the Sophoclean "hero"]

Reinhardt, K. *Sophocles* (Eng trans. Oxford 1979) [demanding but influential]

Scodel, R. *Sophocles* (Boston 1984) [a stimulating introduction]

Seale, D. *Vision and Stagecraft in Sophocles* (London 1982) [focuses on visual aspects and imagery of sight]

Segal, C.P. *Tragedy and Civilization: An Interpretation of Sophocles* (Cambridge, Mass. 1981) [a detailed structuralist account]

Waldock, A.J.A. *Sophocles the Dramatist* (Cambridge 1951) [refreshingly iconoclastic, if often wrong-headed]

Webster, T.B.L. *An Introduction to Sophocles* (Oxford 1936) [old-fashioned but still useful, especially on Sophocles' life]

Whitman, C.H. *Sophocles: A Study in Heroic Humanism* (Cambridge, Mass. 1951) [eccentric but often stimulating]

Winnington-Ingram, R.P. *Sophocles: An Interpretation* (Cambridge 1980) [an outstanding study by a sensitive scholar]

Studies of *Oedipus at Colonus*

Burian, P. "Suppliant and Saviour," *Phoenix* 28 (1974) 408-29 [treats the play as a suppliant drama]

Easterling, P.E. "Oedipus and Polynices," *Proceedings of the Cambridge Philological Society* 193 (1967) 1-13 [a sensitive study of Oedipus' relationship to his children]

Hester, D.A. "To Help one's Friends and Harm one's Enemies," *Antichthon* 11 (1977) 22-41

Kirkwood, G.M. "From Melos to Colonus," *Transactions of the American Philological Association* 116 (1986) 99-117 [emphasizes the local religious setting]

Linforth, I.M. "Religion and Drama in *Oedipus at Colonus*," *University of California Publications in Classical Philology* 14 (1951) 75-191 [downplays religious aspects of the play]

Rosenmeyer, T.G. "The Wrath of Oedipus," *Phoenix* 6 (1952) 92-112 [attacks Oedipus, defends Creon]

Shields, M.G. "Sight and Blindness Imagery in the *Oedipus Coloneus*," *Phoenix* 15 (1961) 63-73